The Source for Solving Reading Problems

Carol Stockdale, M.A.
Carol Possin, Ph.D.

Skills: reading comprehension, language, spelling, handwriting, and decoding

Ages: 5 and up

Grades: K and up

Printed in thc U.S.A.

LinguiSystems, Inc.
3100 4th Avenue
East Moline, IL 61244-9700
1-800 PRO IDEA
1-800-776-4332

FAX: 1-800-577-4555
E-mail: service@linguisystems.com
Web: www.linguisystems.com
TDD: 1-800-933-8331
(for those with hearing impairments)

ISBN 0-7606-0404-5

Author Info

Carol Stockdale, M.A., is the founder and director of the ARK Foundation. The ARK Foundation exists to translate practical tools and methods from the clinic setting to classrooms and homes where students struggle to learn to read. The Foundation, with offices in Tacoma, Washington, provides classes for educators and administrators and produces books and other materials regarding learning disability. Carol was also a founder and co-director of a non-profit clinic for children and adults with learning disabilities. She has taught at various public school levels and has taught college courses for teachers. Her research focuses on the role of visual perception in the acquisition of academic skills, and brings together her interests in visual perception and art and in how individuals learn.

During Carol's sixteen years of clinic work, she developed tools and methods for people who have special learning problems. Shaping memory through symbol stabilization and writing through the use of the learning window are examples of the numerous techniques Carol and others at the clinic developed. She is also an illustrator and a woodblock artist.

Carol received a Bachelor of Science degree from Iowa State University and a Masters degree in Education with an Art emphasis from the University of Puget Sound. She has presented several papers at the International Visual Literacy Association conferences. Her 1977 paper, "A Window to Learning," won the editor's choice award and was published in the conference proceedings. She is a popular speaker at workshops and community organizations that are interested in learning problems.

Carol C. Possin, Ph.D., is a psychologist in private practice in Schenectady, New York, at cpossin@nycap.rr.com. She provides individual assessment and intervention for learning and attention problems, as well as workshops for parents and professionals on these topics. Carol consults with school districts to clarify individual learning disabilities and to assist with intervention strategies for special needs students.

Carol is a graduate of Stanford University and the State University at Albany. She has been a teacher, teacher trainer, school district administrator, professor, and researcher, focusing her work on learning disabilities. She has consulted for school reform projects, such as the Rockefeller Institute of Government, the Education Commission of the States, and the New York State Task Force on Educational Reform. Working with legislative commissions and task forces, she has been instrumental in formulating and passing state and federal legislation and regulations in support of children's services. She has authored books and papers on learning and instruction as well as child advocacy.

Dedication

Our choice of dedication is very simple: this book is dedicated to the children and adults who have challenged us to understand and solve reading problems.

Cover Design by Mike Paustian 📖 Illustrations by Carol Stockdale 📖 Page Layout by Lisa Parker 📖 Edited by Karen Stontz

Table of Contents

Foreword 4

Introduction 5

Part I   Reading Instruction 7

      Chapter 1   Basic Reading...9
      Chapter 2   Spelling—A Skill Linked to Reading 28
      Chapter 3   Handwriting and Motor Skills 37
      Chapter 4   Self-Management of Reading 47
      Chapter 5   Advanced Reading Comprehension 57
      Chapter 6   Independent Reading 64

Part II   Identifying and Solving Problems That Hinder Reading Progress....71

      Chapter 7   The Imagery Base of Comprehension 73
      Chapter 8   Language—Precursor to Reading 82
      Chapter 9   Semantics 91
      Chapter 10 Syntax 98
      Chapter 11 Attention—A Prerequisite to Learning.................103
      Chapter 12 Auditory Discrimination & Memory 109
      Chapter 13 Visual Discrimination & Memory 111
      Chapter 14 Sense of Direction..114
      Chapter 15 Spatial Relations 117

Part III   Appendices—Teaching Tools 127

      1. Symbol Stabilization...129
      2. Sentence Builders/Word Shapes...136
      3. Picture Notes—A Memory Strategy 143
      4. Junk Box 145
      5. Teaching Games 147

Annotated Bibliography..151

Index 163

Foreword

It's difficult to imagine what life would be like without the ability to read. Many of us take reading for granted, relying upon this fundamental skill in countless ways in our daily lives. Conversely, many individuals, young and old alike, struggle to read, thinking it unimaginable that they might ever acquire facility with such skills. Teachers, parents, and others struggle, too, unsure of what's wrong and unsure of how to proceed.

Carol Stockdale and Carol Possin sought to understand the causes of reading difficulty and even illiteracy. As they encountered reading problems, they dauntlessly pursued ways to address them. This book, *The Source for Solving Reading Problems*, grew out of their experiences working with students, who for any number of reasons, could not learn to read.

From my work with Gardner's theory of multiple intelligences, I believe that all students possess strengths that can ameliorate their weaknesses. This book's multi-modal approaches to literacy turn such beliefs into action. Packed with innovative ideas and new approaches, the authors show how to help even the most challenged students become fluent readers. *The Source for Solving Reading Problems* is not a prepackaged program or a teacher-proof curricular guide. Instead, it is an information-rich resource that assists learners in becoming skilled technicians at reading, and assists teachers and clinicians in teaching it appropriately, creatively, and responsibly to the individuals in their care.

Teaching reading is likely the single greatest responsibility of education. Reading introduces us to living; it imparts and extends knowledge; and it allows us to reach beyond ourselves toward infinite possibilities. The work of Carol Stockdale and Carol Possin will assist countless individuals in achieving literacy and, ultimately, the luxury of taking reading for granted in their daily lives.

Linda Campbell
Professor of Education
Antioch University
Seattle, WA

Campbell, Linda. *Teaching and Learning Through Multiple Intelligences*, Allyn & Bacon, 1996 & 1999.

Campbell, Linda. *Multiple Intelligences and Student Achievement: Success Stories from Six Schools*, ASCD, 1999.

Introduction

The Source for Solving Reading Problems was written from our conviction that despite the philosophical debates about reading instruction and the complexity of learning disabilities, reading problems can be clarified and solved. The purpose of this book is to identify for the teacher, clinician, and parent a range of problems that underlie reading failure and to target solutions to those root problems through instructional approaches that help the student remediate or compensate.

The book is organized into three parts. The first part describes reading at basic and advanced levels, related skills of spelling and handwriting, and methods for teaching those skills. The second part describes problems that underlie reading difficulty along with illustrative cases and instructional strategies. Skills addressed in these chapters include imagery, language, semantics, syntax, attention, auditory discrimination and visual memory, sense of direction, and spatial relations. Finally, the appendices offer detailed descriptions of instructional methods and materials that we have found most useful and popular among teachers and clinicians we have trained.

The Source for Solving Reading Problems is a practical book of instructional tools. It is written in everyday language without academic citations and requires no particular background in theory or research to understand. However, it is based on years of reading, research, and applied experience by ourselves and our associates. The ideas have been tested in clinical practice and in classrooms. Previous versions of this book were used to train hundreds of teachers and clinicians. We have seen these ideas work when applied skillfully and analytically to meet the individual needs of each client or student.

We caution the reader not to use this book like a script for teaching reading. We believe that education should be pluralistic. Students should have access to many alternatives that stimulate their growth by meeting their unique needs. Canned programs applied the same way to every student miss the point of this book which is that each student has his own set of reading problems that must be analyzed and solved individually. We merely suggest options for the instructor to consider during the process of analyzing and addressing individual learning disabilities.

Carol and Carol

Part I:
Reading Instruction

Chapter 1: Basic Reading

What is reading? Consider the case of Jack. He can read words, pronouncing each sound correctly. However, he cannot answer any questions about what he reads. When asked what he just read, he says he does not know.

Is Jack reading? No. Reading does not happen in the absence of comprehension. Reading is a matter of bringing meaning to print and getting meaning from print. It is not saying all the sounds. It is not even saying all the words. Reading is comprehension, imposing meaning on the print, gathering meaning from the print, asking questions to exchange meaning with an absent author. Reading is an exercise in meaning.

Prerequisites for Reading: Image, Language, and Symbol

In order to get meaning from reading, readers need a referent or an image for the information that the print conveys. Without this prior knowledge, this image, readers struggle to get meaning from print. They construct and amend their image as the print continues.

Language is also a prerequisite for reading. Comprehension requires that readers interact with the text, asking questions and contributing their own knowledge to the construction of meaning. If readers do not converse with print, understanding may be superficial. This conversation, which is reading comprehension, requires language.

Finally, in order to understand print, readers must be able to control its form. The shapes of language symbols have certain invariant distinctive features. Change the shape of the language symbol, and the message changes. The symbol "g," for example, is different from the symbol "d." The word *mug* conveys a very different meaning from the word *gum*. A student who perceives language symbols inexactly is often unable to gain meaning from print.

Parallels in Language Development

How does a capable person learn to read naturally? Language acquisition provides a useful model for understanding how most people learn to read. Children learn language by immersion in the natural world. Language is not broken up and presented to toddlers in structured lessons of sounds, vocabulary, and grammar. Most children have a natural motivation and capability to learn words and detect the rules of language. They take the

Basic Reading, *continued*

flow of language around them, use their innate abilities to detect important features, and quickly acquire basic language structure and vocabulary at a very young age.

Many children learn to read naturally like they learn language. They detect and remember the important features of written language when they are presented with ordinary language in print. They do not start to read by breaking down printed language into its parts and putting it together systematically. Instead, they notice and learn the sounds of word patterns by themselves without direct instruction. These children can learn to read with ordinary simple print whether or not it is phonetically predictable.

There are other children who will not learn to read efficiently with this approach. They do not learn sound/letter patterns easily. They do not decode and spell words even with repeated practice. These students need a structured approach to learn word patterns.

A New Look at Reading Levels

How can the various reading levels be described? Reading levels have traditionally been described as grade levels like 9.5 or 10.3. Grade level measurement refers to the complexity of the vocabulary and syntax in reading passages used for testing students.

Another way to organize reading level is according to the degree of reader independence. The chart below describes reading from Can't Read (lowest level) to Independent Reading (the highest level). Rank in this system has nothing to do with grade. Even a first grade student may learn to read independently without a teacher.

Levels of Reading

❶ Can't Read Level

- The student may not consistently name letters.

- The student may recognize a handful of words but not without a visual cue present, such as a picture.

- The student may match letters to letters and words to words; however, he cannot identify the written word when he hears it.

Basic Reading, *continued*

- The student cannot decode (sound out) words.

- The student may not have the language for the print—the vocabulary and the syntax.

❷ Beginning Reading Level (reading with external cues such as pictures and teacher hints)

- The student can name letters.

- The student can recognize a handful of words but often needs picture cues.

- The student can identify a written word in a group when he hears it.

- The student cannot make a one-to-one correspondence between print and language.

- The student **may** not have the language for the print—the vocabulary and the structure.

- The student **cannot** pick a book off the shelf and read it cold.

❸ Reading With a Teacher Level (reading with internal cues)

- The student can read the actual language on the page without help.

- The student brings his knowledge to the print.

- The student extracts meaning from the print.

- The student can produce the same language structure that he meets in print.

- The student forms images from the language on the page.

- The student reads for a purpose.

❹ Independent Reading Level (interacting with print)

- The reader interacts with the print.

- The reader asks questions of the print.

- The reader abstracts the argument of the print (of the author).

- The reader can read a variety of print.

- The reader controls the structure of the language on the page.

- The student reads for a purpose.

Basic Reading, *continued*

Students at the Can't Read Level cannot read at all. Students at the Beginning Reading Level do not read without help. The primary difference between readers at the different levels is the type of cue that students need in order to read. *Cueing* is prompting with questions or comments that lead to decoding the print, imaging meaning, and pondering the message. The beginning reader can read with external (teacher) cues. The student at the Reading Without A Teacher Level cues himself internally. That is, he can ask himself the questions that will help find meaning in print. The following sections will discuss methods to help students stuck at the Can't Read Level or the Beginning Reading Level and will describe how to teach students with external and internal cues.

External Cueing

The instructional goal here is that the student who cannot read will learn to read with teacher assistance, that is, with external cues. The teacher gives the student cues in the form of questions and comments while reading with the student. These external cues provide enough hints and supports so that language falls out of the student's mouth during the reading process.

Here are some snatches of teacher/student interaction about the book *The 300-Pound Cat* by Rosamond Dauer. The teacher is cueing the student to participate in meaningful reading.

Teacher: *Do you have a cat? Yes? What is his name?*
Student: *Orbit.*

Teacher: *Why?*
Student: *He runs around.*

Teacher: *Okay. Look at this cat.* (Shows book) *He weighs 300 pounds. How much do you weigh?*
Student: *40 pounds.*

Teacher: *I wonder how he got that big?*
Student: *He ate a lot.*

Teacher: *Probably!* (Teacher reads the title page, turns to the first page of the story, and previews vocabulary.) *Do you know what a* carriage *is? Can you find the word on the page?*
Student: (finds the word *carriage*) *Yeah. It's something a baby rides in.*

Teacher: *That's good. You're good at this.* (Reads the first page of the story aloud to get the student into the flow of the language.) *What happened one weekend?*
Student: (reads) *One weekend he ate...*

Teacher: *...a fancy turnip. And what did he say?*
Student: *He said, "I'm full."*

Teacher: *What did he decide to eat next week?*
Student: (looks at picture) *He decided to eat typewriters. That's...*

Teacher: *...outlandish! So what did William do?*
Student: *He gained weight.*

Teacher: *And what did he look like after a while?*
Student: *After a while he looked a little like a typewriter.*

Teacher: *What happened every once in a while?*
Student: *Every once in a while he ate boots. He looked...*

Teacher: *...disgusting.*

In this example, the student actually starts to read from the book at the notation "(reads)". The teacher's questions and comments keep up the rhythm of the reading. They reveal the harder words and lead the student to use pictures as clues.

If the student is not able to read with the support of pictures and teacher questions, the teacher can start the lesson by overviewing the print first, talking through any new vocabulary, as well as the story sequence as revealed in the pictures. With carefully selected picture books, the meaning is evident, and the teacher can cue the student to guess and read easily.

Which books work best with external cues? Teachers should select books with a strong narrative that makes sense. In other words, the story should be predictable. Also, the pictures should convey the meaning of the story. The vocabulary must be in the students' background, and the level of the books must keep students at the edge of their capability. Books with visually distinctive words and image-based words like *alligator* are easier. Words like *of*, *the*, and *there* are hard. For example, *island* is much more distinctive than *in*, *it*, or *is* and is therefore easier to learn to read.

Basic Reading, *continued*

What makes an external cue effective? Good cues anticipate whatever would trip the student. They fill in unknown words or help the student guess words and read on smoothly. Note in the example on pages 12 and 13 that the teacher anticipates and fills in hard unknown words and language structures and asks questions that help the student guess other words and phrases. Generally, good cues elicit the noun or action words because these words carry much of the meaning of the story. For example: "Who ran?" "What did the cat do?" These are not yes/no questions. They cue actual words in the story.

The reading should flow at a natural pace. The readers do not pause to sound out words. Neither do they stop the flow of the language to correct minor errors that do not alter the meaning of the story. The teacher is very noisy and interested in the meaning while reading along with the student. She maintains the pace by "uh-huhing" and "ah-hahing" as the student reads.

When does the teacher know that she does not need to cue anymore? The student answers this question. When the student looks at the teacher quizzically as though the questioning is odd, cueing can be reduced. The teacher must be sensitive to how much support the student needs and reduce strong cues if the language falls easily out of the student's mouth. External cueing can end once the student can cue himself and read without teacher cues. However, external cueing might be continued to add to the student's reading vocabulary.

How does external cueing work with several students at once? Working in a small group, students take turns reading with the teacher's cues. The entire group tends to become very involved in the reading because the atmosphere is non-threatening and engaging. The teacher provides whatever external cue support is necessary, so the student is always successful.

After reading a book with the teacher, the student can take it home to enjoy privately. Reading the same book several times builds reading fluency. During the next lesson, the student might read a favorite page or tell a summary of the book that the teacher writes down for him to read.

📖 Internal Cueing

In order to move from Beginning Reading to the Reading Without a Teacher Level, the student must learn to read with internal cues. That is, the student must know and implement strategies to help himself when he is stuck while decoding or interpreting the meaning of the text. He has to be able to ponder, question, and interpret in order to interact with the absent author and make meaning of the print.

How can the teacher know that the student is cueing internally? Obviously if the student is cueing himself accurately, the reading makes sense, and the student reads what is actually on the page. If the student is not cueing himself effectively, he comes up with words that are not meaningful and are not predicted by clues in the story or pictures. Both the teacher and the student should recognize inaccurate internal cueing and reread a passage that does not make sense. A student who does not cue himself internally can be taught directly to ask questions of pictures and print. The teacher coaches the student to manage himself when he is stuck.

How can a student be taught to ask questions of print? The goal is that the student will ask for specific information that is answered by the text. If this is difficult, start with pictures to teach the student to ask relevant questions. The teacher shows the student a picture and says, "Margaret, ask me a question that this picture answers." The teacher encourages Margaret to ask good questions, ones that are answered by the picture, guide understanding, and are not answered with "yes" or "no" or a single word. Ideally the questions should be ones that are answered by whole phrases. If the student cannot formulate complex questions, remediation in the syntax of questions may be needed.

For example, the teacher shows Margaret a picture of a cowboy on a horse and says, "Ask me questions that this picture answers." Margaret asks, "What is the cowboy riding? What's the man holding in his hand? What is the horse doing? Where does this take place?" The best questions address important items in the picture, just as good internal cues in reading focus on what is important in the print. To make this point, the teacher can ask Margaret, "What is the most important question about this picture?" Once Margaret can ask a relevant question of a single picture, the teacher can present three visually similar pictures at once and say, "Margaret, ask me a question that only one of these pictures will answer."

Use "Unsticking Readers—Teaching Them to Cue From Within," pages 16-17, to progress from asking questions about pictures to asking questions of print (internal cueing). The student goes from step one to four, one step at a time. *Matching* means that questions and answers are written on separate cards or adding machine strips, and the cards or strips are matched for

Basic Reading, *continued*

meaning. By placing card with card, question with its answer, the student can see that a question is the reciprocal of its answer in form. This is the essence of internal cueing, of asking oneself the questions about print that help make meaning. Good readers cue themselves whenever they get stuck on what they read. Some students just need to be taught directly to cue from within.

📖 Unsticking Readers—Teaching Them to Cue From Within

The process involves teaching student Joe to ask questions that are relevant and specific. He then learns to apply this questioning to print as he reads. The rules of the learning procedure are: do not ask yes/no questions, and questions must be answerable by one picture only.

Joe says and the teacher writes, "The boy is kicking the ball."

1. **Student Joe makes a statement about each picture.**

   "The boy is kicking the ball."

   Teacher Smith writes Joe's statement down.

   She then turns Joe's statement into a question and writes the question down.

   "What is the boy doing?"

   Joe matches the written question to the written statement.

   They repeat this procedure with several pictures.

Joe asks and the teacher writes, "What is the dog waiting for?"

2. **Student Joe asks a question about each picture.**

   Teacher Smith writes down each question.

   She then answers each question with a statement that she writes down.

   "The dog is waiting for food."

   Joe matches the written statements to the written questions.

Basic Reading, *continued*

Small planes are going to Portland for an air show.

> Joe answers and the teacher writes, "The airplane is flying to Portland."

The boy is jumping on a pogo stick.

> Joe asks, "What is the boy jumping on?"

3. **Teacher Smith leads off by reading the print accompanying the picture.**

   She asks questions of the print and writes them down.

   "Where is the airplane going?"

   Joe answers the questions.

   The teacher writes down his answers.

   Joe matches his replies to her questions.

4. **Student Joe asks a question of the print which only the print can answer.**

   Teacher Smith answers.

   In effect, Joe is cueing the teacher!

If the student cannot read the questions and answers required in the above activity, he may need a transitional exercise that helps him read his own language. The teacher asks the student to make statements about several pictures. The teacher writes each statement on a strip of adding machine tape. (If a different color pen is used for each statement, the student won't mix the sentences during the activity.) First the student matches each sentence to the appropriate picture. Then the teacher cuts up each sentence into individual words and mixes the order. The student reassembles the sentence and reads it. Not only does he learn to read known language, but he is also learning about sentence structure.

📖 The Learning Progression

The chart on the following page outlines various reading and writing activities according to the difficulty for the student. External cueing diminishes and internal cueing increases as the student moves up the chart through the levels of the progression.

Basic Reading, *continued*

No Cues: Student Reads Independently

- manages reading comprehension independently when assigned "read page 53"

⇨ writes original composition

Few Cues: Student Predicts the Print Following Learned Methods

- overviews vocabulary on his own
- asks questions and makes predictions alone

⇨ compares and contrasts paragraphs
⇨ paraphrases
⇨ infers information

Fewer Cues: Student Predicts with Teacher Cues

- overviews the vocabulary with teacher guidance
- makes predictions with teacher prompts
- reads to answer teacher and student questions about print

⇨ writes questions and answers
⇨ writes a paragraph or a narrative with teacher guidance

Matches Non-identical Items

- selects *cow* from three words on cards to match a picture
- finds the word *alligator* in a paragraph
- finds the word that is an animal
- reads print that obviously describes the picture

⇨ writes phrases or simple sentences from a picture stimulus
⇨ writes about a picture note

Matches Identical Items

- matches letters to letters ("a" with "a")
- matches print to print (*dog* with *dog*)

⇨ copies letters and words

Note: If a student has difficulty, drop back to an earlier level.

Basic Reading, *continued*

📖 Phonics

Karen's mother homeschooled her because she could not read any of the fifth grade textbooks with her class. Her mother read to her and dictated how to spell each word so that she could "complete" her schoolwork at home. Karen's mother patiently tried to teach her to read simple text each day, but Karen would read the same words wrong the next time that she saw them. She read *pen* for *pin* and *prime* for *prim*. Karen was so discouraged that she shut down after a few errors and avoided reading.

Karen was able to read some text with strong external cues. However, her knowledge of the sounds of letter patterns was so unstable that she had trouble making good guesses as she read. Karen needed help with vowel sounds in particular. Karen and her mother worked with a tutor using a phonics approach to teach Karen to decode the sounds of vowels consistently.

First the tutor noticed that, fortunately, Karen knew her letters. That is, she recognized all of the letters and printed them correctly. If this had been a problem, the tutor would have used a symbol stabilization program described in Appendix 1 on page 129. Karen had to recognize letters consistently in order to go on to the harder task of reading words.

Next the tutor worked with Karen to stabilize the sounds of short vowels. Since short vowels occur in so many words, learning to read them consistently would improve her reading very quickly.

The tutor worked with one vowel at a time until Karen read it correctly in a variety of words and sentences. The tutor did not go on to the next vowel until the first one was stable. Karen spent a week practicing each new vowel with her mother for about twenty minutes a day. The tutor worked with Karen and her mother once a week to construct a lesson plan to be followed at home each day until the next tutoring session.

Here is a sample daily plan for practicing the short vowel "a."

1. Review the sound of "a" by associating it with a word of the student's choice that starts with "a," such as *apple*. The student draws a picture note of "a-apple" that is kept close by to trigger recall. A picture note is like taking notes with a drawing instead of words.

2. The student practices reading words with short "a" using plastic letters on a table. The instructor (teacher or parent) quickly substitutes consonants around "a" to create the opportunity for rapid reading practice by the student—*rat, sat, sap, Sam, Pam, pan, man*, etc. This way the student has an opportunity to learn by making many correct responses. The instructor reinforces the student's response by repeating the correct response after the student reads each word. If the student has difficulty blending the letters in the correct order, the letters can be spread out on the table so that the student is forced to notice each letter and to pronounce each letter slowly in order.

The teacher gradually moves the letters back together in word formation as the student reads the word again. Once the student gains confidence with short "a," the practice words can be lengthened—*chap, tram, bath*, and *path*. Next the student should spell words with plastic letters, and then read and spell words with "a" on paper. Spelling should be learned in conjunction with reading, as described in Chapter 2: Spelling—A Skill Linked to Reading, pages 28-36.

3. While reading books using external cues, the student notices words with short "a." Very soon the instructor expects the student to cue himself internally to notice short "a" and read such words correctly.

Note the order of difficulty:
- reading with plastic letters
- spelling with plastic letters
- reading words on paper
- writing words on paper
- increasing the length of words and sentences to read and spell

Finally the student reads words with "a" correctly in text that may still be presented with external cues.

Basic Reading, *continued*

A similar lesson is practiced for each of the other short vowels, usually one new vowel per day or even per week with built-in review of vowels already learned during previous lessons. Once the student knows more than one vowel, review can involve substitution for the vowel sound in words as well as for the consonants—*tap*, *tup*, *pup*, *sup*, *sap*, and *sack*, *suck*, etc. The instructor can line up plastic letters on the table vertically and move consonants down the line thus to create rapid practice.

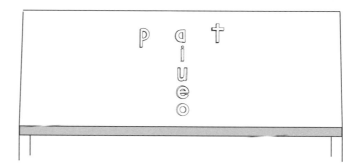

Try to make real words, but do not worry about occasional made-up words. They allow students to practice decoding unfamiliar words. Also students often find made-up words silly, and humor brightens the lesson.

What if the student mixes up vowels, such as "a" for "e"? Check to make sure that the student **hears** the difference between the sounds made by the two vowels. Pronounce words beginning with "a" and "e" and have the student point to and say the sound of the vowel that begins the word you are pronouncing.

Instructor says,

Student points to and pronounces,

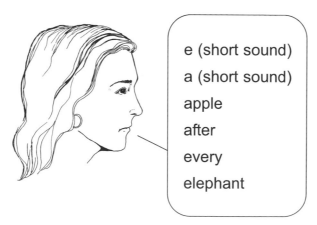

Instructor says	Student points to and pronounces
e (short sound)	e
a (short sound)	a
apple	a
after	a
every	e
elephant	e

Move on to words with short "a" and "e" in the middle position:

bet	e
bat	a
sent	e
fence	e

Usually students can learn to distinguish between sounds with one session of this sound discrimination practice or with practice repeated over several days. The occasional student who cannot learn to discriminate between two sounds will have to rely on visual memory for whole words to learn to read the sounds in question.

The student often needs similar lessons with plastic letters to learn long vowels, contrasting the long vowel with the short vowel.

Although long vowels usually do not require as many days of practice as short vowels, you should still present only one new vowel at a time. The student can usually discover and verbalize a rule for long vowels. It might be something like, "With a vowel, a consonant, and a vowel, the first vowel says its name." Once the student can read a long vowel with plastic letters, he should move on to spelling with plastic letters and then to reading and writing words and sentences on paper. During reading with external cues, he should be expected to notice independently more and more long vowels as they occur in print and to decode them correctly.

Whenever another problem with sound/letter correspondence occurs repeatedly, the instructor can present practice opportunities similar to the lesson outlined here. Such problems might occur with consonant blends (*tr*, *spl*, *sp*) or vowel combinations (*oi*, *ai*, *ou*).

Basic Reading, *continued*

Phonics presented as isolated sounds can be repetitive, boring, and an unnatural way to read. Notice how quickly the student is guided to reading sentences and externally cued text in the lesson on pages 16-18.

📖 Visual Phonics

Visual phonics is phonics taught with an emphasis on visual memory for words and letter patterns.

Most people recognize words and letter patterns by their visual features, and they learn reading quickly, sometimes even without help. With other children, no matter how many times they study a word, they do not remember it. These students must be taught directly how to hold a visual image (i.e., the shape of a word) in their memory.

Reading requires that a person image the visual configurations of words, and words that have greater visual distinctiveness are easier to read and spell. Notice the shape of words like *apple*, *Washington*, or people's names. The shapes of these words are distinctive and memorable for most people, but if a person's visual memory for these features is inaccurate, reading is poor.

Distinctive features of words are like distinctive features of people's faces. One might remember that Aunt Florence has a certain shape of nose. It only takes a glimpse of that nose to trigger the recognition of Aunt Florence. In other words, we recall words like the faces of friends. We learn to read a word by recognizing it as a familiar face and linking that face to its meaning.

People who read and spell inaccurately do not recognize the distinctive features of words like the "e" on the end of *store* or the double "t" in *rattle*. These features cluster in families like *battle*, *prattle*, and *cattle*. The teacher can help students recognize these families and learn a common feature of a cluster of words rather than learn one word at a time.

Students who do not remember visual features of words can be taught to do so. Students can learn to draw a "picture note" that triggers a spelling pattern. For example, a hill drawn over the letters "ill" or a snail drawn around "ail" may trigger memory of these letter patterns. A good picture note triggers both the meaning and the sound of the pattern and focuses on the distinctive features of the pattern. However, it is not necessary to include the letters in the picture note. Simply linking a sketch of a golf club with the word *golf* can help the student recognize the word in print and spell the word. Each student must create his own personalized picture notes and adjust them until they trigger recall because memory is individual.

The process of drawing picture notes for word family patterns should be carried out in a language rich environment to clarify understanding and to create multiple memory associations. The teacher and the student should engage in a great deal of discussion while drawing the notes. Here are some ideas for engaging students in this process.

The teacher can give students 30 word cards representing about **three** letter patterns, such as "ale," "ight," and "ack." The teacher asks the student to sort the cards into groups or families. This is a discovery process. The student needs time to discover and verbalize similarities. The teacher uses language during this discussion to help sort words and create associations in memory to the words.

Word Cards

male	lacked	night
tackle	sale	backed
tale	sighted	baled
paler	black	sack
kale	brightly	Jack
flight	tighter	track
gale	delight	right
fighting	shale	rack
package	frighten	stacking
whale	might	stale

Sorted

• male	• night	• lacked
• baled	• sighted	• tackle
• paler	• brightly	• backed
• whale	• flight	• black
• shale	• tighter	• sack
• gale	• delight	• Jack
• kale	• right	• track
• tale	• frighten	• package
• sale	• might	• stacking
• stale	• fighting	• rack

While sorting, the teacher and student discuss the spelling patterns—their spellings and their sounds. The student can draw a picture note for each pattern that is hard to remember. The teacher can mix the word cards and:

- have the student sort again by picture note

- ask the student to read the picture note

- ask the student to read the word cards

- ask the student to give a word orally that belongs to a given family

- ask the student to give a family that belongs to a certain word

- ask the student to spell a word

Once a student knows the family features of words like *sail*, longer words like *sailor* are easy. *Sailor* only requires reading two more letters.

During this practice, detecting and clearing up any ambiguous understanding of word meanings is important. It is difficult to read and spell words with fuzzy meanings.

How much visual phonics is necessary?

About 25 word-family patterns are sufficient to provide a solid base of words that are consistently recognized and spelled. As far as which words to choose, longer words should be included because they are distinctive and therefore easy to learn.

What is the instructional procedure for visual phonics?

Each word is written on a separate index card. The teacher selects three families of cards, like the ones on pages 26 and 27, and mixes them thoroughly. They are spread out on a table. The student sorts the cards into families, while identifying each word family. He draws a picture note to reinforce his memory for the word pattern if he has difficulty remembering the pattern.

25 basic word families:

ave	ill	ake	ing	ance
brave	chilly	mistake	singer	balanced
shaver	pillow	milk shake	jingle	glance
save	spill	bakery	morning	allowance
knave	gorilla	makeup	bring	entrance
bravery	hillside	awaken	zinger	advance
crave	village	cupcake	kingdom	dancer

ade	eat	ock	ump	ice
lemonade	meat	socks	jumping	mice
shade	beaten	blockade	umpire	device
fade	seated	clock	trumpet	rice
trade	eaten	socket	stump	suffice
parade	wheat	knocking	crumple	price
barricade	cheated	rocket	plump	nicely

ook	all	atch	ound	ight
hooks	tall	scratch	around	fighter
booklet	wallet	matches	found	tonight
looked	tallest	mismatch	rounded	mighty
cooking	falling	catcher	greyhound	lightning
mistook	baseball	hatchet	pounded	knight
crooked	balloon	hatchery	ground	delightful

able	tion	act	ain	ink
table	traction	fact	painful	thinker
movable	action	actor	complain	stink
comfortable	dictionary	exactly	remainder	sinking
fable	vacation	tractor	explain	blink
cable	prediction	practice	entertain	thinking
stable	fraction	react	maintain	winked

itch	ide	ell	ate	one
switch	tide	yellow	later	lonely
pitcher	beside	cellular	grateful	stone
itchy	sidewalk	dwelling	create	telephone
kitchen	wider	umbrella	celebrate	postpone
stitches	hide	propeller	locate	alone
ditch	bride	telling	plate	boned

What can be done about words that do not belong to families like *was* and *the?*

Students can usually read these odd words once they learn a bank of family words that provide context around the unknown words. Teaching these words directly is necessary only if the student is confused about them. In the context of so many family words rich in meaning, these words should come easily.

In conclusion, reading can be taught in a logical progression from external to internal cues. Phonics can be used when sound/letter correspondence problems impede word recognition. Visual phonics allows the student to expand reading vocabulary rapidly through the acquisition of whole families of words. The role of the educator is to be a thoughtful observer of the student and to guide the student with a method that works for him.

Chapter 2: Spelling—A Skill Linked to Reading

📖 What is Spelling?

Spelling is writing words accurately at any time. It is not simply success on a spelling test. One can cram for a spelling test and get 100% but spell poorly when doing day-to-day writing tasks.

📖 Why is Good Spelling Important?

Spelling is important because it is a marker of quality communication and caring about the reader. Misspelled words on a job application do not win a job.

Spelling improves the clarity of the message. Spelling errors can distract the reader and distort meaning.

Knowing accurate spelling is important because it permits a person to be an efficient writer. A large spelling repertoire promotes easy access to words for written composition. On the other hand, meager spelling skills can block even bright students when they try to get their good ideas on paper.

> Computerized spell checkers do not catch all errors!
>
> **Computers due the words I no knot.**
> **There feets our grate four one and awl.**

📖 What Words Must Students Know How to Spell?

Students need to know their personal vocabularies well enough to write freely with them in composition. Also there are special lists for certain disciplines, jobs, and interests like sports. Some careers and subjects, such as biology, have greater spelling demands than others do. A doctor spells medical terms; a machinist, mechanical terms; and a salesperson, the names of her products and her customers. An individual can be a competent professional despite poor spelling skills if she has secretaries or other support staff. She is, however, dependent upon such support.

Spelling—A Skill Linked to Reading, *continued*

📖 What Learning Abilities Support Spelling?

Visual Memory

Some people have poor visual memory for letters and words. They may mix the order of letters, reverse the direction of letters, substitute one letter for another, or omit parts of words. Visual memory is an important factor in accurate spelling. In order to spell accurately, one must examine what was written, compare it to visual memory for the word, and edit.

Auditory Memory and Word Segmentation

Spelling is also supported by good auditory control. When a person hears or says a word to be written, the auditory stimulus triggers the visual memory of a word. That is, a person with good auditory memory can hear or tell herself a word to spell, hold it in auditory memory, and visualize the word while writing it.

Some students do not hear sounds correctly. They may fail to distinguish between certain sounds like short vowels in *bit* and *bet* or *bat* and *bet*. If students cannot distinguish between sounds after careful practice, they may need to use a visual approach to spelling.

Some students have difficulty segmenting words into component sounds. For example, they do not hear *slap* as four sounds in the correct order, "s - l - a - p" and cue themselves to write the letter corresponding to each sound. Strategies for word segmentation include the following:

- Anchor the vowel sound to a known word with the same vowel. Discuss the similarity. "This is 'a' as in *apple*."

- Spread plastic letters apart. Gradually move them together to illustrate the construction of words from component sounds.

s	l	a	p

- Use backward buildup. Start pronouncing a word with the vowel sound and the word ending and build backwards.

a ⇨ ap ⇨ lap ⇨ slap

Motor Memory

Motor control for writing symbols like letters and numbers also supports spelling. Motor control makes practice easier so that students are more motivated to practice. Also, for a person with good motor control there is a distinctive feel to writing words with rhythmic pattern like *cheese*, *school*, and *wiggle* that makes spelling them easy. There is actually motor memory for spelling so that writing a word several times improves spelling memory. People who have difficulty with handwriting may lack motor memory for spelling and are often poor spellers when writing. Writing words over and over does not help them. They may, however, spell better orally.

What Learning Must Precede Spelling?

Letters must be stable. This means that students must be able to name and write letters the same way every time. In order to focus on spelling a word, students must know how to form the letters in the word easily. Otherwise they are distracted from the spelling task by the inability to form letters efficiently.

What does it look like when letters are not stable? Students may misname letters. Also they may forget how to form letters and construct them anew each time. With these students the teacher will notice that they form the same letter various ways. Sometimes they may start at the line and other times they may start at the top of the letter. Sometimes they may link the letter to other letters, sometimes not. Inexact letter memory means writing is a very laborious and inefficient process.

Students must be able to read a word before spelling it. If they cannot, it is not possible to read and edit what they spell. Learning letters and reading precede spelling.

Spelling—A Skill Linked to Reading, continued

How to Analyze a Student's Spelling Problems

Start by examining a student's errors:

- Is the problem with sight words?

- Does the learner mix up letter order, confusing *schole* with *school* and *slpat* with *splat*?

- Does the learner leave out parts of words, usually the middle parts?

  These errors indicate visual memory problems.

- Does the student misspell phonetic words? Unfamiliar words?

- Does the learner have problems with vowels or with other sound/symbol correlation? With word endings or middles?

- Does the learner mispronounce and then spell like the mispronunciations, such as confusing "pre" with "per"?

  These errors indicate auditory memory and word segmentation problems.

- Is the student's handwriting sloppy and inefficient?

  Poor penmanship may indicate weak motor memory.

Attention problems may also account for some of these errors, such as leaving out or misspelling parts of words like middles or endings.

Strategies for Helping the Poor Speller

For students with poor auditory, visual, and/or motor memory, deliberate cognitive strategies can make spelling easier. Coach students to focus these strategies on words that they consistently miss. Students need to sort words into "absolutely know" and "don't know" groups. They need to focus their study on the "don't know" group. Another wise step for students is to read back what they wrote and check for errors. Some spelling strategies are listed on the next page.

Spelling—A Skill Linked to Reading, *continued*

1. **Learn sound/letter linkages directly if the student does not know them and is able to learn them easily.** Sometimes students simply have not learned the sounds of some letters and letter combinations like short or long vowels, "oa", "ch," or "igh." However, if the student does not readily grasp phonics, move on to other instructional approaches.

   Here are some ideas for teaching phonics:

   • Try using three-dimensional plastic letters. Use lowercase letters, of course! Who reads and writes with all capitals?

   • Teach one sound/symbol (like short "a") at a time until it is stable as detailed in Chapter 1. Do this by having the child read short words that you form rapidly by moving around plastic letters on a table.

   • Have the learner spell words with the same sound/symbol by moving the plastic letters.

   • Finally have the student read and write words and words in sentences on paper. If the student has difficulty making the transition to pencil and paper, an intermediate step is possible. Have the student see the printed word on paper, select plastic letters, carry them across the room, and then build the word with the plastic letters. This requires the student to retain the visual image of the word in memory long enough to reproduce the spelling. Then the student can walk back across the room and write the word on paper.

2. **Learn to spell words in families, and then learn to tie new words to families that are already known.** Students need to learn to notice word families (e.g., *sight*, *right*, *mighty*, and *delightful* or *brave*, *crave*, *bravery*, and *knave*), and use this strategy on their own to reduce the number of words to learn. The word-family approach reduces the memory task to learning one family pattern rather than every word in the family.

3. **Apply special techniques to homonyms like *meat* and *meet*.** Make homonyms visually distinctive by coloring the key portion of the word that makes them different ("ea" vs. "ee").

   This strategy points out the difference between similar words and may solve the memory problem. If there is still difficulty remembering whether to write *meet* or *meat*, use additional strategies tying the appearance of the word to the meaning. For example, you eat meat, and *eat* is found in *meat*. Also the two "e's" in *meet* are shaking hands. You are applying **imagery** and **story** to distinguish homonyms in memory.

4. **Practice recognizing and creating "stuck-together" words like *sportsmanship* and *nevertheless*.**

5. **Learn words with hidden letters by saying the hidden letters while spelling the words.** For example, pronounce the "l" when writing *salmon* and the "ch" when spelling *yacht*.

   s a l m o n

6. **Learn prefixes and suffixes.** Students can start by sorting words on cards by prefixes and suffixes, such as "pre" words and "per" words. Once the student has sorted words into categories and knows the meaning of the prefixes, the student can use prefix meaning as a tool to spelling.

7. **Look for words in words, such as *wed* in *Wednesday*, *nun* in *pronunciation*, and *era* in *literature*.** Students do this more easily when they have previously found and created "stuck-together" words.

8. **Make stories out of words.** The *angel* has *gel* in its hair. You *spit* on *al* in the *hospital*. Does *science* have a *conscience*? *All* straight lines can be *parallel*.

9. **Make picture notes out of words to create memory cues.** For example, draw eyes (oo) on the o's in *look*. Then generalize this cue to other members of the family such as *book*, *cookie*, and *rookie*. Draw a "t" in *hatchet* to look like a hatchet to cue spelling of "tch" words. "Tch" words are then referred to as "hatchet" words as the family name.

10. **Make the word into a picture or line pattern that emphasizes the shape of the word as a memory clue.**

    • Draw around the word to make a picture shape.

    boat   hill   alligator

- Draw long and short lines to represent letters in words.

11. **Practice spelling "monster" words using large motor movement on a vertical surface.** In spite of strategies and practice, some words are still difficult. Use erasable pens on a window or chalk on a blackboard. As the student writes each letter, she should say its sound or the letter out loud, whichever she can do. She needs to read the whole word out loud after writing the letters. To make the transition from large motor spelling on the vertical surface to pencil and paper on a desk, the student can reinforce her memory by writing the word in space with two fingers in several locations around the room. Of course, this only works if the student can formulate firm motor memories. Finally the student writes the word on paper at the desk.

    Once students have tentatively learned a monster word, parents or teachers can promote overlearning by asking them to write the word in the air several times a day. This allows for frequent, spaced practice. Occasional interruption of activities to write *bureau* in the air can become humorous and fun.

12. **Keyboarding helps some students spell more accurately.** Students who have motor-planning problems that interfere with handwriting may spell more correctly when using a keyboard. However, the student who cannot recall the visual appearance of a word will not find keyboarding very helpful. Even if the spell check indicates many words are incorrect, the student may not know how to change them.

Application of Spelling Strategies

Students may **know** spelling strategies but not remember to **use** them routinely. They can practice using spelling strategies with learning tools such as the spelling box or spelling notebook.

Spelling—A Skill Linked to Reading, *continued*

Spelling box: This device for managing spelling words stresses strategies for recall. The student has a box with dividers such as the ones commonly used for fishing equipment. Most students need six or more compartments. A lid of heavy cardboard is cut to fit over the compartments. A narrow slot just large enough to slide in a slip of paper is cut into each section. The student labels each slot with a spelling strategy. New words are put on slips, the preferred strategy is selected, and the word is inserted into the corresponding slot. The student should be rewarded for choosing appropriate memory strategies as well as for retaining the correct spelling of a word. Therefore, credit should be given for choosing a suitable method for remembering the word.

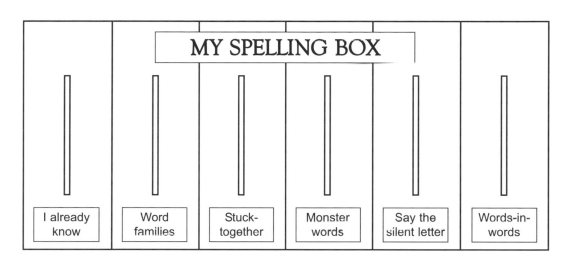

MY SPELLING BOX

| I already know | Word families | Stuck-together | Monster words | Say the silent letter | Words-in-words |

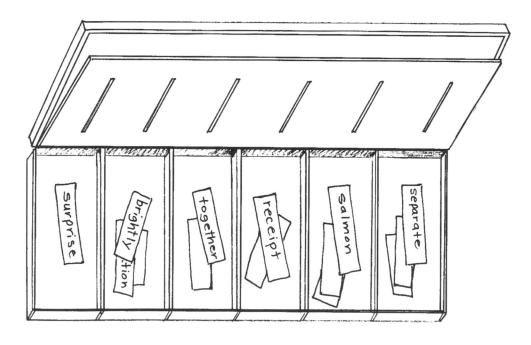

Spelling notebook: The spelling notebook is very similar to the spelling box except that the format is different. The student lists her preferred strategies in a notebook with a space beside each. This master sheet can be duplicated to form a reference book that can be used throughout the year. Students discover the strategies that are most effective for long-term recall. Eventually most students center on three or four favored methods.

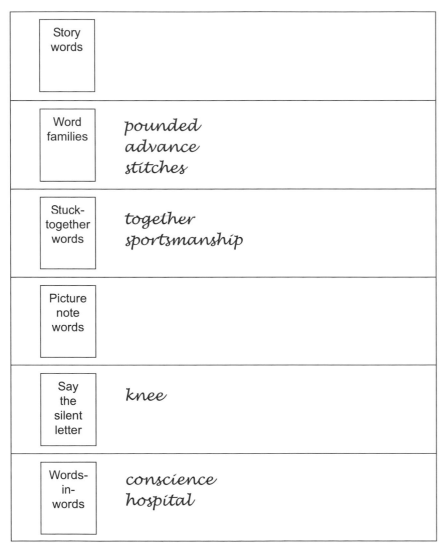

Story words	
Word families	*pounded* *advance* *stitches*
Stuck-together words	*together* *sportsmanship*
Picture note words	
Say the silent letter	*knee*
Words-in-words	*conscience* *hospital*

In conclusion, students are far more likely to be engaged in using spelling strategies if they can see their progress. A visual display of known words can provide this encouragement. Known words can be put on a ring, kept in a spelling box, or written in a notebook. Each of these methods allows the student and teacher to review known words occasionally and to monitor progress.

Chapter 3: Handwriting and Motor Skills

Handwriting supports reading. It reinforces the memory for letters, for words, and for sentence structure. Students with good motor memory for the shape of letters and words will often learn to read and spell new words by writing them.

The degree of emphasis on handwriting, the form of scripts, the type of handwriting instruction, and the timing of that instruction have varied greatly throughout history. During earlier times, the author's "hand" was an indicator of education and refinement. Hours of practice with a carefully shaped quill produced flowing, graceful script for the educated few. Overlapping circles ( ) and continuous vertical lines ( ) marched across pages of practice drills.

Today's crowded curriculum allots limited time to penmanship. Also, handwriting instruction currently differs widely between regions, districts, and even classrooms in the same building. Rarely do children spend much time in drill and practice. Furthermore, computer word processing has greatly diminished the value placed on handwriting. Even so, most students learn to write legibly during the primary grades of school. However, there are students who struggle with handwriting, often despise copying, and avoid or shortchange classroom assignments that require written responses. Students who cannot form letters efficiently are overwhelmed when asked to write a whole paragraph.

📖 Writing Instruction

Most kindergartners are introduced to manuscript writing (printing). Even this first script can take several forms. The "stick and ball" method of forming letters is a popular method. The child learns to stroke down from the top to form the stick (↓) and draw circles from the top (⟲). Some letters, such as "c", "u," and "h," require the circles to be left open. Others, such as "g" and "j," require a curved end to the stick.

D'Nealian, another form of manuscript, is a curved form of printing taught in many schools. D'Nealian letters look more like cursive writing and may create a transition to cursive when it is introduced later in the third or fourth grade.

Handwriting and Motor Skills, *continued*

Learning any style of handwriting is a challenge. Children often mix capitals and lower case, form letters backwards, or even reverse words or groups of words. For most children, this confusion gradually lessens with study and practice. For them, any method, if consistently practiced, eventually seems to result in legible handwriting produced at a satisfactory rate.

However, some children do not become competent at handwriting. The label *dysgraphic*, which means *cannot write*, is often applied to them. They never learn to write clearly and efficiently. In fact, some are unable to write more than a few words or an awkwardly produced signature. Still others can write, but the process is slow with labored pencil lines carving grooves across the page. Fatigue reduces their handwriting efforts to a few lines. Other children write in staccato fashion as they stop to recall one letter or word form only to lose the memory for the next one.

Why Handwriting Is Difficult

Motor problems: Some children have motor difficulty. These individuals have problems with many fine motor activities, such as cutting with scissors, buttoning buttons, drawing, and, of course, handwriting. They may recall the shape of a letter perfectly, but actually making the pencil form the shape is awkward and troublesome.

Motor problems are marked by handwriting that is hard to read and that deteriorates rather than improves, even with tutoring. Sometimes when there are motor problems, letters eventually fall down and collapse on the line. With uneven pressure on the page, there are fewer features included in each letter, and the letters are jammed together. By fourth or fifth grade, these students usually write minuscule letters with their fingers at the tips of their pencils.

Motor problems affect the memory for letters and words. With inconsistent motor movements, the brain does not create a strong memory of the movement used in forming the letters and letter sequences. Therefore, letter formation is not automatic and requires effort. Each "g" may be like writing "g" for the first time. Consequently, the student must exert conscious visual control to write, which is fatiguing. For the student with motor memory problems, writing is somewhat like the average person trying to write with the non-dominant hand.

Handwriting and Motor Skills, *continued*

Most individuals form clear motor memories that allow an activity to become nearly automatic. They can write while looking at the board or glancing at the book. Their bodies "know" the motor movements required to form each letter. A child with depressed fine motor skills generally does not develop such clear memories. In fact, his motor memories form slowly and may remain inexact. With careful concentration, his handwriting may start out looking accurate. However, this level of focus is difficult to maintain. Soon physical fatigue sets in, and his handwriting quickly deteriorates.

Large motor problems may also contribute to writing delays. The effect is more subtle and individual than fine motor problems. Large motor difficulty affects the student's ability to maintain erect posture, to sit comfortably in a seat for extended periods, and to continue an activity without undue fatigue. Large motor problems divert the student's energy from handwriting to maintaining body position.

Inability to recall letter formation and letter order in words: Some students, including those with dyslexia or visual-spatial problems, cannot remember exactly the appearance of letters or the order of letters in words. Since they cannot recall how a word looks, they cannot rely on internal images to guide their pencils as they form the letters. Does the line loop forward or backward? Is the "b" or the "d" the letter with the ball first? Is the "m" three bumps or two bumps? Such tenuous and fleeting visual memories undermine handwriting for the dyslexic student. Handwriting is a precision activity. Quite often children who have dyslexia or visual-spatial problems are inflexible about the shape of a letter. For example, the letter "t" when first learned as a straight stick (†) may no longer be accepted as a "t" when the bottom is curved (t). Similarly, "y" may not be accepted as "y" when the tail is curved (y). This inflexibility complicates reading or writing different scripts. Changing scripts to learn cursive writing may be very difficult.

Inability to recall the spelling of words: Some students have a generalized inability to recall the appearance of words that goes beyond letter order or vowel confusion. They spell very poorly. Some of these students have phonics skills that they rely on whether or not a word follows a phonetic pattern. They tend to pour their energy into letter formation writing *wuns*, *wauk,* and *agin* without noticing that these words are not phonetically spelled and must be recalled as visual patterns. Other students with poor visual memory for the spelling of words also lack phonetic ability and are literally stymied. They may be able to copy words or a sentence from a book or the board, and they may even be fluent when allowed to dictate words, ideas, or stories. However, because of their inability to recall the appearance of words, they cannot write down their own words.

Word-finding problems: Sometimes what appears to be difficulty with handwriting is actually a language problem. Students who have word-finding problems typically produce limited quantities of stereotypic language. They may not have handwriting problems. In fact, they may be successful with copy exercises. Their inability to recall words leads them to produce brief, formulaic compositions such as the following paragraph by a fifth grade girl.

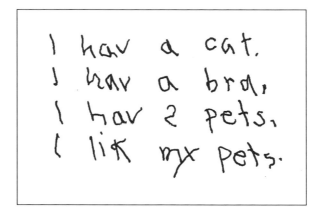

This girl's word-finding problems also limited her ability to dictate sentences or stories. She needed to work on imaging words in order to form clearer memories and improve word recall. (See Chapter 7: The Imagery Base of Comprehension, pages 73-81.)

📖 Strategies

For many students, handwriting problems are very persistent; they do not go away. In spite of expert instruction and conscientious practice, some people will always write poorly. Their writing should be accepted as long as it is legible, and they should not be criticized or penalized for a disability that cannot be completely overcome.

When problems are recognized in a young child, steps can be taken to ease the process of learning to write. Usually students benefit most from a combination of remedial instruction and accommodation that reduces their dependence on manual writing.

Handwriting and Motor Skills, *continued*

Educators should evaluate handwriting problems and determine whether motor deficits, visual-spatial deficits, or both are affecting the student's ability to write. The following lists of behaviors describe and distinguish between motor and visual-spatial performance.

Motor-Planning Behaviors	**Visual-Spatial Behaviors**
Can the student:	Can the student:
• draw accurately (pencil control)	• find routes without getting lost
• use correct motor movement to form letters (Which letters are problems?)	• copy letters and words accurately
• form letters accurately (Which are problems?)	• sort patterns and shapes accurately
• sustain writing with energy	• sequence events in time
• write on the line	• use capitals and punctuation accurately
• write neatly	• spell non-phonetic words accurately
• write with spacing	• draw accurately (visual recall)
• write willingly	• perform evenly in math, especially place value, fractions, and geometry
	• use and draw maps effectively
	• remember locations; not lose things

A person with motor problems can image an "m" clearly but not write it well because of clumsy fingers. In contrast, a person with visual-spatial problems may not image an "m" accurately and may be unsure where to send the pencil when forming it. Both persons may form "m" poorly, one because he is clumsy and the other because he is unsure of how an "m" is supposed to look. A person with both motor and visual-spatial problems is very disadvantaged when writing or drawing: he may not know what an "m" looks like, and his hand does not work skillfully to form one.

Handwriting and Motor Skills, *continued*

The distinction between motor and visual-spatial problems helps fine-tune expectations and instruction in order to meet different student needs. People with motor problems tend to tire during writing tasks. Their written work should be broken into short intervals, and they should be given alternative ways to express themselves, such as with a keyboard. Their instruction should include guided motor practice. In contrast, people with visual-spatial problems can usually write longer because they do not tire so easily. However, motor practice will not help them very much. They need instruction in imaging, that is, forming accurate images of where to send the pencil. (See Chapter 7: The Imagery Base of Comprehension, pages 73-81.) People with visual-spatial problems usually have ongoing problems with copying and spelling, and they often need a spell checker.

1. **Develop the language to describe shape, position, and motion.**
   If students do not know this language, it should be taught before proceeding to other steps. They need to know specific vocabulary that describes shape, position, and motion in order to understand the instructional language of letter formation.

   - Shape: square, triangle, circle, diamond, rectangle, cube, cylinder, cone

   - Position: above, below, beside, over, under, across, diagonal, vertical, horizontal, parallel

   - Motion: loop, cross, dot, forward, backward

2. **Teach cursive immediately.** Since initial memory traces are very persistent, the student who struggles with writing is usually unable to change scripts from printing to cursive. Therefore, skip printing and go right to cursive if handwriting is a severe problem. Cursive is usually easier than printing.

3. **Teach handwriting in large scale.** Large motor movements are easier to perform accurately and are more memorable for most students. Therefore, letter formation should be introduced with large arm movements.

Handwriting and Motor Skills, *continued*

A Learning Window can serve as an instructional surface for large movement handwriting. This is a framed plastic window on a stand. The vertical surface is easier to use than a horizontal one. The teacher stands on one side of the Window and guides the student on the other side. The student writes or draws from left to right. The teacher on the other side of the window writes or draws in the opposite direction at the same time.

The teacher's guidance includes modeling both the movement and the verbal script (words) that describe the writing. Modeling the movement helps the student who has insufficient motor control learn the motion. The student's pen follows the teacher's pen from the opposite side of the window. Modeling descriptive language (e.g., "I go up and around.") helps a student develop scripts to guide her pen as she makes a loop independently. Students need to develop their own descriptive language for the motions. This becomes their script.

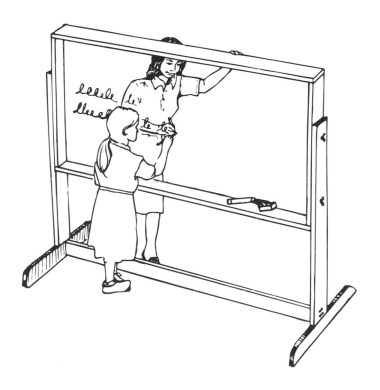

"To make an *ℓ* or an *e*, start in the valley, swing up to make a loop, and go back down to the valley."

Writing backwards and right to left is easy to learn if the teacher has a guide. Make a guide by writing the alphabet on a clear plastic sheet and then turning it over. This can be copied and reduced in scale to a convenient size. The starting place for each letter should be clearly marked. The teacher can hold this as a cue card for herself.

Handwriting and Motor Skills, *continued*

 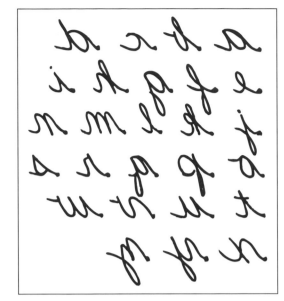

The order of instructing letters is determined by the natural progression of the strokes used to form them. As soon as two or three letters are learned, they should be practiced as clusters and words. One letter progression that has proved effective is:

el   le   t i j   jell   tile   u w
we   ul   f s   fuse   cad   qq
n   m   o b   boo   hk   pr
x v   y z   you   as   book   dog

The ease or difficulty of each stroke is usually apparent as the student forms the letters. The exercise needs to continue until each letter can be readily created. As he writes, the student must not lean on the board. His arm must be free to form the large-scale letters accurately. The goal of the exercise is to create basic motor memories for the letters. These memorics can then support him as he goes on to write in smaller scale on paper at his desk.

4. **Reinforce letter memory with spaced practice.** Ask the child to form the letter with large movement in the air. For instance say, "Make me an 'm' on the door, on the ceiling, on the floor." The student makes an "m" with large sweeping movements each time. Once the movements are done accurately, the teacher and the parent can ask the student to make an "m" in the air from time to time throughout the day. This spaced practice becomes a humorous way to reinforce letter memory.

5. **Teach selected accommodations.** Students have the right to accommodations when their disabilities impede learning with typical instruction. These rights are protected by disability law and apply to all age levels. Despite extra effort, both handwriting and spelling remain inefficient skills for some students. They need alternative routes for expression. The following accommodations may be necessary for handwriting and spelling problems:

   - **Cue sheet:** Often a small number of common words are especially difficult for students with spelling problems to recall, blocking the smooth flow of ideas onto paper. Students can make cue sheets of troublesome words to tape on their desks. Often words such as *they*, *there*, *they're*, *their*, *them*, *what*, *that*, and *these* are confusing both to read and to write. The students may need to add picture notes beside some words on the list to distinguish them. These cue sheets are useful accommodations to help students express their ideas freely.

   - **Dictation:** Some students need to dictate language for another student or an aide to record. This is especially important when the task involves time limits, such as tests. Such an arrangement needs to be set up ahead of time and rehearsed. Students need to learn methods for organizing their ideas so that the dictation reflects their knowledge and ability.

   - **Editor for composition:** A student for whom handwriting is very hard work often must place his major focus on the act of writing. He needs to get the words on paper without worrying about commas and quotation marks. Later he can go back and edit. These students often benefit from a list of priorities to address during the entire composition process such as:

Handwriting and Motor Skills, *continued*

❶ Decide on what I want to say.

❷ Put it down on paper.

❸ Read my words to see if I said what I wanted to say.

❹ Look at my mechanics.

Of course many students will need more detailed planning at various phases of the process.

- **Keyboarding:** Like handwriting, keyboarding is a motor skill, but with major differences. Keyboarding strokes do not involve the continuous change in directions that handwriting does. Nearly all students, even the truly dysgraphic, can learn to use a keyboard if they approach the task wisely. Because initial motor memories are so persistent, efficient fingering patterns need to be begun before "hunt and peck" has taken over. Moreover, students should rehearse the correct fingering regularly until the motor memories are in place. Establishing reliable motor memories is very difficult. Sufficient time must be allowed. Many dysgraphic students take two or three times as long to learn the keyboard compared to most other students. Once learned, however, the skill can usually be performed at a high level. In the computer age, handwriting disabilities can be reduced to an inconvenience.

6. **Use oral-entry word processing.** Software is available that allows writers to speak into the word processor, which then prints what was spoken. This is a useful accommodation for people with spelling and handwriting problems.

Chapter 4: Self-Management of Reading

Students need to manage themselves. Self-management of reading is essential for establishing and achieving personal goals and for becoming a successful student. However, many students have difficulty progressing to self-management. Consider the following cases:

High school junior Bonnie failed tests frequently. She would study for hours and still fail, never knowing what she did wrong. She would complete every daily assignment correctly, and yet she would fail a test on the same material. She said she was using good study skills like restating the material in her own language and asking questions of the material. Bonnie was a quiet student. She did not seek help with her study problems.

Fifth grader Josh could decode words, but he could not understand or remember a story. He would remember random fragments, not making connections of sequence, cause and effect, or comparison. Also he would recall the less important words or ideas if they were the most visually distinctive. He did not recognize what was important to remember. Josh was a leader in athletics, but he did not participate in class. He did not volunteer answers, and he avoided the teacher's gaze during discussion.

Third grader Mark had some reading skills, but he misread obvious sentences. For example, if a boy in a story showed his mother a box, Mark did not guess that she would ask what was in it. Also he would misread the meaning of text even when pictures on the page described the action clearly. When Mark's teacher gave him easier assignments well within his capabilities, he played with items in his desk or talked to his friends instead of doing his work.

📖 Learning Self-Management of Reading

Bonnie, Josh, and Mark were not managing their reading. They were reasonably able to do what was necessary to read, but they were not telling themselves to execute the necessary actions. They were not initiating reading strategies. Managing reading is telling oneself to take appropriate steps to make meaning out of print. Some people call this using executive functions or using internal cues as opposed to external teacher cues. People need to manage their reading actions like a boss directing people.

In the first case, Bonnie was not analyzing the defects in her study process and correcting them. Actually, she was failing because she was reviewing orally for written tests, and the leap from conversational oral practice to written production on the test was not working for her. She could not interpret the written questions, which were in academic print language, not conversational language. She joined a study group that tried working with written questions and practicing answers in writing. After rehearsing with written questions, she received a B+ on the next test.

The point here is that Bonnie had to manage her study situation in order to succeed. A student at her age must become a self-advocate instead of waiting for Mom or the teacher to tell her what to do. She has to analyze her problem and do what works. A student who manages her own study asks for what she needs, such as oral tests, written practice, or extended time. Bonnie asked for written practice. The good test results encouraged her to be more assertive. She adopted a new body language: she sat up more and more, looked people in the eye, and asked for what she wanted.

Josh also needed to learn self-management of his reading. He had some reading tools, but he was not using them. He avoided class participation out of embarrassment over his poor performance. The teacher worked with him privately. She helped him learn to create an image of an event in print and to use images of story events to visualize and remember sequence in a story. First the teacher asked him to read small story chunks and make a picture note of the event in that chunk. (A *picture note* is the student's own quick sketch of something that cues memory of a story event.) Once he had a picture note for each of several story chunks, the teacher had him use these picture notes to cue himself to tell the story in correct order. Soon Josh made picture notes regularly on his own. One day he arrived at reading class without picture notes and said he did not need them because he could see the sequence of events in his head. Other students might never reach this point. Josh took control of his reading comprehension, and he understood his own self-management behavior that worked.

Mark was also not managing his reading. He could certainly tell what action pictures depicted, but he was not telling himself to use these clues while he read. He also was not using his reasoning to make good guesses about what people would say or do next in the story. Managing reading takes effort that Mark was not putting forth. Coached by a teacher after school, Mark began to prepare himself for reading a story by looking at pictures, asking questions of the text, and predicting the story ending in order to construct the logical direction of the story. When he engaged in

Self-Management of Reading, continued

these behaviors without teacher prompts, he had assumed management of his reading comprehension.

Problems with self-management are common. Sometimes students do not know what they know and what they do not know. They do not think of testing themselves to know what they know. They may not think of initiating the questioning and analysis necessary to understand what they read rather than just decode words. They may think they know how to read to study for a test, but they do not read efficiently and effectively so as to remember. They may not be aware of how many tasks or what complexity of tasks they can handle when they plan their studying. They may not know their attention limitations and how to compensate for them. In sum, without a well-developed executive function, they simply do not manage their reading.

These students may succeed when the teacher directs their learning, but they do not direct themselves. Self-management of reading is an important goal. Students need to learn to read effectively without the teacher telling them what to do each step of the way.

Some students do not manage their reading because they do not think of doing so. Others do not choose to manage themselves because the payoff is not there or because doing so takes too much effort. Students have to choose to take charge. They need encouragement and support for their efforts to read independently.

Activities That Foster Self-Management

1. **Teach the student to control feelings that block learning.** Sometimes students are too anxious or discouraged to learn, and they may not even be aware of these feelings. If emotion is a major dominating factor or if nagging by the teacher or parent has created deaf ears, a control scale can be useful. It is a tool for teaching students to identify feelings, related behaviors, and their language labels. This scale is comprised of ten stairsteps that describe both actions and the feelings that accompany each control level. The teacher and student build the scale by working together to develop appropriate descriptive words for each step. The student identifies where she is on her scale. "I'm at a two in history. I flunked the test and feel sick to my stomach." The teacher and student then identify what actions to take so the student can move up one step. The student can also choose a level at which she is comfortable and work out a method of achieving that level.

Self-Management of Reading, continued

The scale has several advantages. Control is centered in the student. The scale helps the student sort behavior from feelings so that negative feelings do not block actions. The scale also helps the student perceive levels of feeling and action. Students who learn to differentiate feelings from actions can understand and control themselves better. They anticipate their own feelings and take actions to stay in control. Also, they understand other people's feelings and relate to them more effectively.

Look at this control scale below, from "bad & sad" at the bottom to "cool" at the top. Each individual student would fill in personal descriptors for each step.

Control Scale

Feelings		Actions
_____ cool _____	10	best work — top grade
_____	9	_____
_____	8	_____
_____	7	_____
_____	6	_____
_____	5	_____
not so worried	4	did part
worried	3	try to start
panic	2	do nuthin'
bad & sad	1	sit

Self-Management of Reading, *continued*

2. **Gradually fade external cues for word identification.** If a student does not figure out how to manage her own reading independently or with minimal teacher guidance, the teacher can tell the student directly what to do and gradually withdraw teacher prompts so that the student takes on the role of manager. Teacher prompts are called *external cues*, and the student's self prompts are called *internal cues*. Strong external cues tell the student precisely what to do. Weak external cues give the student only a hint. A student using internal cues tells herself what to do.

A teacher should attend to the level of support to give a student, with a goal that the student will use internal cues. The following student actions take place with cues of decreasing strength.

Strong external cues for the early reader

- reads the word *rabbit* with a picture of a rabbit beside it
- reads the word *rabbit* with a picture note cueing the word
- matches the word *rabbit* to the word *rabbit* in an array of words
- picks out *rabbit* from an array of three words, with *rabbit* being the only word that starts with "r"
- picks out *rabbit* from an array of three words, all of which start with "r"

Weak external cues for the early reader

- finds the word *rabbit* on a page when the teacher says, "I'm looking for the word that talks about an animal"
- reads the word *rabbit* when the teacher says, "This is a story about Peter Cottontail."

Internal cues for the early reader

- finds the word *rabbit* in print on her own
- reads the word *rabbit* correctly when coming across it in a real life situation.
- writes the word *rabbit* in a natural situation without cues

The cues in this list become less direct and controlling as one moves down the list. If, at any point, students cannot respond with internal cues alone, then the teacher must go back to using external cues to support the student. However, the student needs to go beyond highly supported instruction and reach the goal of independent, self-managed reading. This is the essence of managing one's own reading. It is reading without outside support.

3. **Cue comprehension of whole passages.** With more complex reading tasks, like comprehension, the teacher matches the appropriate cue level to the student's needs in a similar manner, starting with external cue support as needed and aiming for student self-management. For each of the following examples of comprehension exercises, the teacher can adjust the level of the cue as needed.

The student can learn specific actions, such as the following, to increase comprehension of reading passages.

• Predict from pictures what will happen in a story, looking for characters and sequence of events. The teacher asks, "What do you think will happen in this story?"

• Predict the specific language of print from pictures and the logic of the story. The teacher asks, "What are some of the words you think you will find in this story?"

• Periodically stop the story and recap what has happened so far.

• Make up one's own reading comprehension test questions about the story.

As stated above, the teacher can create external cues of various strengths to guide the student in learning to execute each of the above strategies. For example, if the teacher wants the student to predict story outline from pictures, she can teach her this strategy with a strong external cue by asking what happens in each picture and then directing the student to put the events in several pictures together. After doing this with a couple of stories, the teacher might ask the student approaching a new story what she should do first with the pictures. At a later time, the teacher can ask the student what she should do first without mentioning the pictures. Eventually, the teacher watches to see if the student cues herself internally. If she does not, the teacher can ask if the student remembers what she should do when she starts to read a story. The goal is that the student will use picture cues effectively on her own.

Cueing at the wrong level is a mistake. The cue can be too strong. If the student already uses a reading strategy independently, she will be both bored and frustrated by external cues. Another danger is not providing the student with enough support. If the student does not use reading strategies independently, it is discouraging for her to be assigned work that requires this capability. Examples of fading teacher cues too quickly

Self-Management of Reading, *continued*

include assigning a new reader a story to read without preparation, or assigning homework that requires application of new and difficult concepts that were never explained in class.

Miscalculating the support level can cause failure and resentment among students. For example, demonstrating the concept or process on the board before assigning homework is not enough for many students. They usually need to rehearse the material or the strategy in class with teacher supervision before practicing alone with homework assignments.

Students learn to recognize when they know something, and they can decide when they are ready to do a homework assignment. Saying so themselves puts students in the position of managing their learning. Students can also say when they are ready for a test and will do so readily when they are confident that they know the material or process.

Students should be coached and encouraged to be their own advocates as in the example of Bonnie. They need to ask for background information and alternative materials before starting a new unit, they need to find help from their peers, and they need to ask for additional support when they need it. Students who solve their own reading problems should be commended.

4. **Teach self-talk.** Students can be coached to direct themselves with their own speech before internalizing this control and coaching themselves silently. They might learn to say something like, "Let's see, first you describe one thing, and then you describe the other, and then you look for what's different between the two. That's contrast." Self-talk hearkens back to an earlier stage of human development. Young children often talk themselves through a task. Adults also use self-talk when a task is difficult.

5. **Teach the student to identify the overall organization.** An important management strategy for reading is to look for the overview of a story or a chapter. At all levels, students must be aware of this key to comprehension. The teacher can coach students to follow these steps.

   • Look at the ending of the story or chapter first.

   • Find the main point of each section.

   • Link each key point to its location in the outline of the story.

Students need to identify the main points and their sequence. Teachers can cue students to do this and then expect them to practice it themselves.

6. **Teach self-evaluation.** How can a student evaluate her own self-management? She can create a rating scale to evaluate herself. With the teacher's initial guidance, a student can set up criteria to determine how well she is controlling her own learning. She can rate herself and ask her teacher to rate her.

One student, Marianne, made up the management rating sheet below.

I want to make the following changes over the next six weeks. The teacher and I will rate me from 1-5 (poor to excellent) on each item below once a week to help me understand how well I am managing my learning.

1. Read the material one time and understand and remember the main points.　　　1　2　3　4　5

2. Decrease the amount of time needed each night to do homework.　　　1　2　3　4　5

3. Anticipate the questions that will be on the tests.　　　1　2　3　4　5

4. Predict the results of a test accurately (good or bad and tell why).　　　1　2　3　4　5

5. Decrease the anxiety I feel on tests.　　　1　2　3　4　5

This is only one example of a form to rate the student's management of her learning. The student should produce one that rates the precise elements that are of concern to her. What is important is for the **student** to develop the form with some help from the teacher as needed. This is, after all, an exercise in self-management.

7. **Empower students.** Why is empowering children to manage their own learning so important? Control leads to feelings of self-efficacy. An empowered person approaches life assertively, solving problems or acquiring the necessary outside help to solve them.

Self-Management of Reading, *continued*

Giving children permission to make choices and live with the consequences empowers them. Parents and teachers of students with learning disabilities may have great difficulty giving this permission. Their desire to "save" the child results in shifting control of the learning away from the student. A parent who worries about homework might arrange to find out the assignments directly from the teacher, work with the child to make sure the homework is completed, and check it over for mistakes. Although the child has completed the homework, she did not really take responsibility for it. The "savers" must step back and give the student permission to take over if the empowering process is to be successful.

What are some ways to give students control? One way is to respond positively to a student's request for control. One student, Julie, a seventh grader with learning disabilities who had successfully completed a semester of math, was assigned to a different teacher for the second semester. Knowing that she needed to stay with the teacher who understood her learning style, Julie went to the office, found out the procedure to change teachers, filled out all the forms, and talked to all the required counselors. In a few days, she was reassigned to her former teacher.

Another way is to allow children to set markers for themselves. For example, they can decide that when they have read the chapter and made up their own tests for the chapter, they will be ready for the classroom test.

Empowerment can make a vital difference in a student's response to frustration. One who does not take an active approach to learning might give up, saying, "I can't do this; it's too hard," or "Do it for me." In contrast, an empowered student will ask, "What do I need to do?" and "How can I do it?"

How can you make homework assignments specific and yet more empowering? Consider the power given to a high school student in the following homework assignment on reading a story:

- Read the story and ask questions of the reading. Be a teacher. Ask the questions the teacher would ask. Ask questions at different levels:

  ❶ literal and data specific
  ❷ inferential
  ❸ abstract

Self-Management of Reading, *continued*

- Identify the author's point of view in three steps:

  ❶ Identify the events.
  ❷ State the author's opinion on the events.
  ❸ Look for the thesis statement.

- Paraphrase what you have read. Stop reading whenever you feel overloaded and paraphrase the language.

- Allow the print to trigger imagery within you. When you feel a sense of overload, you are losing the image.

- For convoluted language, go directly to the heart of the sentence and stop the language. This means identifying the focus in a sentence or paragraph by finding the key subject and verb. This is a useful remedy when complex text feels overwhelming.

Self-management can be attained gradually one step at a time. It is limited by developmental level and attention capability. (See Chapter 11: Attention—A Prerequisite to Learning, pages 103-108.) Students will learn to manage their learning in some subjects or parts of some subjects long before they demonstrate broader control. Growth in management skill is fundamental to long-term academic and personal success.

Chapter 5: Advanced Reading Comprehension

Comprehending difficult text is more than understanding words and sentences. The reader applies interpretation and reasoning to the whole text to move beyond literal understanding.

Consider the case of Julie, a college freshman. The harder Julie worked in her freshman classes, the more she failed. She stayed up until 3:00 a.m. each night writing volumes of notes. When she did not know the answer, she studied longer. She reread her books, copied over her notes, and memorized more and more details.

Julie focused heavily on detail. For her, studying an English novel meant looking up over 50 vocabulary words, writing out lengthy definitions, and memorizing them. During class discussions, Julie volunteered to participate and always had some detail to drop into the discussion. Her tests and papers required that she answer broad questions. When the professors returned her papers to her, they usually had written on them "missed the point" or "you did not answer the question." Julie knew that something was wrong, but she could not understand her problem.

Consider also the case of George, a high school student. George wrote beautiful, flowery, structurally correct sentences. However, his writing did not get to the point or answer a question directly. He would respond to a short answer question with pages of writing. Sometimes the teacher would find the right three-word answer accidentally in his lengthy response, and he would get that item correct.

George said he did not know why some answers were right and most were wrong. When he was asked to discuss a story, he said that it was about whales, and that was all he could say about it. When the teacher asked him to describe the plot line (actor and action) or to compare and contrast, George did not answer.

What is the problem here? These students have plenty to say, but they just do not seem to get it right.

Julie was stuck at the lowest level of knowledge: rote learning. Her study time was a ritual of reading, note taking, and memorizing. When she failed a test, her solution was to memorize more details. While Julie succeeded in many of her high school classes at the literal level, college required complex thinking skills. She had not learned to analyze, synthesize, and evaluate her reading.

To clarify, analysis is taking reading apart to understand its structure and logic. Synthesis is putting together multiple ideas and drawing new conclusions. Evaluation is critiquing against a standard that one may first have to create. Julie needed to approach her college reading with this depth and quality in her thinking, not to devote more time to learning details.

Julie needed to interact with print rather than learn it by rote. She needed to stand back from her reading, analyze elements such as theme and structure, and compare them to what she already knew. She needed to read actively and reflectively, working over the material in her own language and questioning the author.

George was similar to Julie. He read on a literal level with no critical thinking. He had no paradigms to analyze complex print. He simply did not know how to structure the analysis of a story or a poem, so he wrote whatever came into his mind about it.

Memorizing, repeating back, and getting the "right" answer require lower order thinking. Reading with higher order thinking is more active. It involves discussing and analyzing from different points of view and creatively linking new ideas in print to other knowledge. The critical thinker analyzes concepts, theories, and explanations; questions the meaning and implications of print; and compares the print to what he knows.

Teaching Reading Comprehension

Students like Julie and George come to teachers with a history of problems and a set of skills that are highly individual. No single instructional approach will help all of them. Observing students and reacting to their problems with unique and appropriate solutions is the key to their instruction. Here are suggestions that may be useful:

1. **Address basic skills issues first.** Reading for complex analysis may be exceptionally difficult for a student who struggles with basic skills, such as decoding words. When a student's basic skills are not automatic, energy is exhausted during the early stages of reading comprehension, and the student may never get to the step of analyzing text. The first question to ask then is whether the student needs help with basic reading skills before moving on to analysis. In the meantime, the student can interpret easier books, books on tape, or film.

Advanced Reading Comprehension, *continued*

2. **Teach writing to read.** Students become critical analytical readers as they learn to write. Therefore, reading and writing should be taught simultaneously. As students write, they must figure out the distinctive characteristics of the type of writing that they are producing. They come to understand firsthand how an author writes an essay or a poem. They learn the language and structure of print, which they can then use to question and challenge the authors that they read.

3. **Teach perspective taking.** For people who lack perspective-taking skills, complex reading is very difficult. A good reader must understand the author's viewpoint from clues in the print, even though the clues may be subtle. He also examines a story from the viewpoint of each character. Perspective taking is developmental and cannot be expected of very young readers. However, an effective advanced reader often shifts perspectives and uses expressions like "on the other hand," "from this other character's viewpoint", and "if the main character had not done such and so." Flexibility and openness to multiple viewpoints are essential characteristics of the advanced reader.

    To practice perspective taking with print, the teacher can ask the student to add to a story begun by a classmate. Next the teacher can ask the student to tell a story about Sam, Harry, and Elvis from Sam's point of view and then from the viewpoint of the other characters in narrative print. Finally the student should practice recognizing and describing an author's point of view.

4. **Teach students to take charge of print.** Students need to manage print rather than be intimidated by it. They can take command in several ways. First they should have permission not to read something. If they evaluate a book as poor, they should have permission to put it down. Students may take different viewpoints and argue with the author, and students have a right to their own viewpoints. Students also learn to rise above print by questioning it, changing the outcome of the story, or reading about the historical and cultural context of the print to understand it more deeply. The goal is to demystify reading and promote the confidence that is necessary to relax and reflect deeply while reading.

5. **Teach guidelines for analysis of print.** Encourage the student to construct a set of steps for approaching a particular kind of print. While the teacher may help the student do this, the student should construct his own "recipe" or script and practice using it on increasingly difficult material. If a student cannot remember a long or complex script easily, he can keep a written copy of the guidelines to use as needed.

6. **Teach guidelines for argumentative print.** With argumentative print, the student needs to learn through discussion and example what this type of writing does. The author has a certain point of view and his goal is to convince the reader to see things his way. The student must learn to identify the thesis and track the argument. Starting with simple examples where the thesis is evident, the teacher can present the student a series of questions. The student can alter these questions to construct his own analysis guidelines.

   • *What is the author's thesis?* What is he trying to convince you of? Identify the thesis; where is this statement in the print?

   • *Evaluate the thesis.* Is it arguable? Do people care about it? Is the thesis qualified? Does it avoid universals like "all" and "every"? Does it use qualifiers like "smoking is related to lung cancer" rather than sweeping generalities like "smoking kills"? How many times has this thesis been stated already? What is the merit in saying it again?

   • *Examine the argument.* What kind of argument is it—deductive or inductive? What kinds of evidence does the author use: statistics, scientific arguments, expert opinions, emotional appeals, historical evidence, or eyewitness accounts? Is the evidence valid? Does it relate back to the thesis? Is anything missing that would make this better argumentative writing?

7. **Teach guidelines for story.** A film or a familiar fairy tale that can be analyzed without reading it is a good place to begin. The teacher and student work together on a series of questions that the student eventually molds into his own guidelines for analyzing fiction.

   • *What are the focuses or central events that structure the story?* State each focus in noun-verb-noun form, and then examine your list of noun-verb-noun statements as the plan of the story. For example, Miriam meets girl; girl invades home; etc.

- *Which focus is the complication (first focus) and which is the resolution (last focus)?* The *complication* is whatever happens to complicate the life of the main character, and the main character is the one who changes the most. The *resolution* is what happens that resolves the complication and must be accomplished by the efforts of the main character.

- *What is the plot point (the turning point)?* The plot point in the story is the "aha!" where the character realizes what he must do. The plot point is the window that reveals the theme of the story. It is the point where the reader should be able to figure out the theme.

- *What is the theme of the story?* Examine the changes in the main character and the meaning of the plot point.

- *What is the author's intent?* Why did he write this? What was he trying to teach?

Through practice with the teacher, the student can create his own guidelines for reading and understanding other forms of analysis such as comparing and contrasting or describing a process. With a brief set of steps to follow, the student can practice and produce most basic forms of analysis. For example, to compare, the student describes one item and then the other. Then the student identifies what is common between the two descriptions. While they seem obvious to many people, some students do not figure out such guidelines for themselves. However, they usually can construct them through discussion and practice with a teacher.

8. **Teach students to image print.** Visualizing print clarifies understanding and makes analysis possible. (See Chapter 7: The Imagery Base of Comprehension, pages 73-81.)

Imaging helps the reader peel away symbolism and abstraction to reveal the central idea. A key problem for students like Julie and George is that they are literal readers. They miss the underlying key point and get stuck in details on the literal level. They do not see through the details to what is being stated indirectly.

To understand narrative text, the student needs to detect its structure by imaging key points and their sequence. The teacher can start by having the student identify the key point in a sentence, which is usually the actor-action-object. For example, consider the sentence, "The black horse, frightened by the loud noise, galloped home with an empty saddle." Selecting the key words (actor = horse, action = galloped, object = home), helps the student get to the meaning. The student should draw a picture note to help clarify and remember this key point. Next the student does this same exercise with a larger chunk of reading, a section of a story or a chapter. Sequencing the picture notes for story chunks helps the student visualize and remember the order in the story or chapter. Finally the student should identify the main point of a whole chapter or story.

9. **Teach imaging to clarify.** It is not enough to run one's eyes across the print and define words with words. The reader needs to see the image that the words describe, like playing videotape in the mind. Imaging is especially essential to understanding descriptive print. The text may be symbolic: "Mary gulps down novels." To understand a symbol, the reader should be able to draw the image of such a descriptive piece and then check understanding by comparing drawings with those of other students.

Poetry requires special skill in visualization because a poem does not convey the entire image directly. The key to understanding poetry is not in memorizing labels or jargon like "iambic pentameter," but in visualizing the image that the poet is suggesting. For example, the phrase in Sandburg's poem, "The fog came on little cat feet," triggers the image of quiet stealth. This image suggests the meaning that fog, like a cat, can steal unseen into one's presence.

Visualizing the overview of a chapter in a textbook is an important study technique to prepare for tests. The student can depict the key ideas on one sheet of paper by diagramming in either words or picture notes. An example of this procedure from a chapter on the atom follows. The arrangement of the key ideas in the atom diagram on the next page shows spatially the outline of the chapter in three parts.

	The atom:		
	basic structure common to all atoms	various kinds of atoms and how they differ	altering atomic structure

The student identifies the key points above and fills in important details under each key point.

Able students are assumed to develop this imaging skill automatically as they progress through secondary school and prepare for college. However, many students, especially those with atypical learning patterns, need to be systematically instructed in these methods of advanced reading. Imaging is a fundamental step in text analysis and is necessary for academic success.

Chapter 6: Independent Reading

Even independent readers have problems. Their most frequent issues are reading to enjoy, reading to remember, taking tests, and reading to research. Each of these will be discussed in the following sections.

📖 Reading to Enjoy

Many students have never enjoyed reading. To help them, the teacher can ask them to go to a bookstore and pick out what they would love to read. If they cannot do that, the teacher can give them something wonderful to read and have them read a part of it. Students will be more motivated if they have their own purpose for reading and if this purpose is verbalized. Teaching to the student's motivation is illustrated in the following story.

The Snake in the Jar Method

Standing just outside the door of the classroom, nine-year-old David scowled at the teacher who motioned for him to enter. "Why don't you teachers just give up on me?" he blurted out. "I'm never going to learn to read." Grace Faunce shook her head. "I'm not giving up on something I haven't tried yet," she replied. "Come on in and tell me about yourself." She closed the book on her desk and waved him to a chair. Knowing the importance of beginnings, especially with a child like David, she had made sure no other children were scheduled in the resource room that morning. As they chatted, she skillfully guided the conversation to discover his interests. David displayed his knowledge of the farm animals that he cared for and the wild creatures inhabiting the woods to the north of their farm. His eyes lit up when he described the snakes and lizards living there. Making himself as invisible as possible, he had followed some of them and discovered where they lived and what they ate.

The light in David's eyes was just what the teacher was waiting for, although she would have preferred a different topic! The next day, when David reluctantly arrived at the classroom door, he encountered a large jar containing a coiled tan and black snake. Beside the jar lay a book about snakes opened to a picture of a similar snake. As Grace had taken the jar from her brother, the biology teacher, and carefully piled books around it in the trunk of her car to keep it from falling over, she muttered to herself, "If anyone had told me this is what it would take to teach reading, I would have quit right then!"

David studied the snake for a few minutes and announced, "I know what this is. It's a bull snake. I found one in the barn last week." Mrs. Faunce looked, shook her head slightly, and pointed to the book. She continued to work with another student. David looked at the snake, then at the picture, and finally at the words under the picture. Suddenly he whooped, "I've got it! It's a hognosed snake. It's darker than a bull snake, and it eats toads! I saw one eat a whole toad once!" He looked up. Mrs. Faunce smiled and nodded. Slamming the book shut, he shouted, "Oh, no you don't!" "I didn't," she answered, "but you did, David. You read! Now we have a place to start. This book is just full of snakes for you to learn about."

By this time in his school career, David had been subjected to many hours of drills and flash cards in the attempt to help him unlock the mysteries of the printed word. What he needed, however, was a reason to read. When he found out he could get answers to his questions from the words on the page, he was hooked.

When discussing print that students have selected, the teacher has a variety of options. She can ask them what they like and what they do not like about it. They can take different viewpoints and argue with the author. They can also change the outcome of the story. Students need to read the material in the context of when it was written and the author's situation at the time. The idea is to control the print rather than have it intimidate the reader.

The teacher's role is important to this process. Reading is not what the teacher has the student do; it is what the teacher does **with** the student. The student and the teacher should read the same piece together, each bringing questions and comments to the ensuing discussion. The discussion is then an honest exploration of genuine questions and observations. The teacher models her own curiosity and value for learning, and she shares her willingness to be vulnerable to ideas with the student.

The teacher should not ask students to read something that she would not read. Students should have permission not to like what they read and not to finish the selection if they evaluate it as poor. As a result of this exposure to excellent writing and honest discussion, students usually end up in bookstores looking for more.

📖 Reading to Remember: Studying for Tests

Reading is an important way to learn. Students who have trouble remembering what they read can be helped. The important point is to look for the structure or argument in the material to remember. Extracting the outline of an argument and restating it briefly imposes meaningful order on the print and reduces the memory load.

The student can practice reading to remember by placing a question about each key point in the reading on a sticky note and placing the sticky note on the text section that answers the question. Later the student lifts these notes and sorts them into "know" and "don't know" piles. For "don't know" questions, drawing a picture note to trigger recall usually helps. This systematic study process focuses attention directly on what the student needs to know but does not know.

An ineffective test taker does not strategize her study; she reviews with ritualistic activities, such as looking at notes or writing them over. The effective learner identifies what she needs to know and focuses study on the part that she does not know.

It is also helpful to reduce the amount to remember. Organizing knowledge into a few categories can do this. The student asks herself what categories of information will be on the test and what goes into each category. Usually this information can be reduced to one side of one sheet of paper which becomes the focus of final study before the test.

The student needs to practice three kinds of test questions: literal, inferential, and abstract. The following examples will clarify the meaning of each of these types of questions.

- *Literal:* "What is the cowboy riding?" The question asks for information that is stated directly in the print.

- *Inferential:* "Where is this taking place?" The answer to this type of question may be inherent in the print but not stated directly. The picture may include a cactus, or the print may refer to "sand in the cowboy's boots." The reader must bring some knowledge to the print and analyze the content to answer the question.

- *Abstract:* "How would you compare the individualism of the cowboy in America to that of the herdsman in Mongolia?" This task requires abstraction, analysis, and synthesis of information, usually information beyond the print at hand.

The student needs to anticipate the type of question that will appear on a test and practice it. The reason why many students succeed on high school tests but not on college tests is that the latter tend to have more abstract questions, and the student does not anticipate and practice this type of question.

The teacher can coach the student in strategies for approaching test questions. For example, the student should learn to jot down all idea words on scratch paper until a thesis statement emerges. The student places order on the argument, and only then the student writes.

A common type of question involves definitions of key words. Preparation for this type of question must include identification of new vocabulary words and building images for them. Picture notes are recommended. (See Chapter 7: The Imagery Base of Comprehension, pages 73-81.) Drawing the meaning of a new word requires identification of its distinctive features, and the picture note triggers memory.

Often the feelings associated with test taking are the problem, not writing the test. Telling a student not to worry usually will not work. Test-anxious students may need desensitization. They need to practice responding to "formidable" abstract questions in writing. If severe anxiety about tests persists, the student can rehearse alone in a comfortable room with the teacher, then rehearse in the library, and finally in a classroom. Gradually the student approaches the most threatening test situation.

Reading to Research

Students need mentors to show them the inside ways to research. A teacher can go to the library with students and teach them the details of how to use it as a researcher. A key point is introducing the student to the resources that professors use, such as academic background books.

As far as conducting their own library research, people with learning problems often do not know where to start. As a result, they may not start at all. They need to learn how to build a structure for the research process. The following steps can guide library research.

Independent Reading, *continued*

❶ The student begins by asking questions. What does the student want to know about a topic? The student writes each question on a separate card. If the student cannot ask a minimum of 10 open-ended questions, she does not have sufficient background to proceed. She can either gather more background or change her topic.

❷ The student then sorts or groups her cards into categories of topics and ideas. The student evaluates each of the categories. Does researching this topic really matter? If not, discard it. Do more questions within the category need to be added?

❸ For the topics that remain, the student reads in the library what other people have written. She continues to add and subtract topics. At this point, the student should still be accepting ideas.

❹ At some point soon, the student comes to a thesis, structures an argument, and orders the topics. A visual map of the argument may help. It should be reducible to a page. Soon information gaps become obvious.

❺ Additional research focuses on these information gaps. Sources should be flexible—books, journals, videos, and interviews. The teacher should help the student figure out who would have the needed information. A student must also learn to evaluate what she knows and what she needs to know next.

❻ The writing should be done topic by topic. It is not a question of writing the whole paper at once, which can seem overwhelming. The teacher can give the student a model paper with a thesis statement and main parts clearly marked. Having this example to follow can sometimes help the student with organization problems.

❻ Writing should be done with a clearly stated intent, and it should be evaluated for whether the writer got that message across. The teacher can mentor writing with intent. The student verbalizes her purpose, such as convincing the reader that smoking endangers health, and proceeds to write quietly in the teacher's presence. The teacher can model doing the same. They both write, and the only sounds are the pens scratching across the pages. Afterwards, they read each other's pieces to see if each got her intent across.

Independent Reading, *continued*

This suggested research/writing process emphasizes asking genuine questions and writing the research report with a true purpose.

In conclusion, suggestions for helping advanced readers or any student with specific learning problems are not meant to be followed exactly. They should be applied creatively and appropriately to meet the needs of individual students.

Part II:
Identifying & Solving Problems That Hinder Reading Progress

Chapter 7: The Imagery Base of Comprehension

Benjamin read and reread the Social Studies chapter on Western Expansion and the Louisiana Purchase. Despite his efforts, nothing stuck in his mind. The next day during the test, he could not define "Western Expansion" or give arguments for and against the Louisiana Purchase in an essay question. He did not **see** the chapter content clearly in his mind. He needed to image the words and text clearly and specifically in order to understand and remember efficiently. Without this understanding, Benjamin was trying to remember too many ambiguous words by rote. Such a task was impossible.

📖 Imaging Defined

Imaging is forming a mental picture of meaning. It is visualizing a peacock when using the word *peacock*. Although images are often in the form of visual memories, they include other perceptions as well. People remember how things sound, feel, and smell.

Clear, detailed images enrich understanding and enhance memory for the words that label the images. To illustrate, try learning the names of insects you have never seen. Then try remembering the names while looking at the actual insects or pictures of the insects as you notice what is distinctive about each one. Learn the names of the insects as you observe them. Notice that once the images are clear and specific, it is easier to remember and use the words for these images.

Difficulty with imagery is a significant learning problem. Fuzzy images lead to ambiguous word meanings and limited vocabulary. Severe cases of vocabulary deficit described here illustrate the roles of imagery and language comprehension in reading.

📖 Cases of Imaging Problems

Consider the case of Jacob, an eighth grader, who was cooperative but very reluctant to talk. When asked a question, he often would not respond. Jacob had good motor skills, as demonstrated by his achievements in sports. He also liked to draw, but he limited his drawings to stereotypic cartoon characters. He became upset when the art teacher asked him to draw real objects from memory because he could not remember them in detail.

Even though Jacob scored average on intelligence tests, he struggled with his schoolwork, especially with difficult reading texts. On a language test, he scored average on grammar, but low on vocabulary. While he was answering the vocabulary questions, he scored low on homonyms, and his word definitions were vague, touching on one aspect of a word's meaning but not the essence of the word.

A problem with imagery is often misdiagnosed. For example, 30-year-old Darlene was mislabeled "retarded." Conversations with her were impossible for most people to understand. When she telephoned her teacher for help with her homework, all Darlene could say was, "Stuck!" Her teacher responded, "Hi, Darlene. Is that you?" "Yeah." "Are you having trouble?" "Yeah." "Where is your paper?" "Right here." "Remember the last time you were here we were talking about pictures?" "Yeah, pictures." "Remember we were asking questions?" "Yeah. Make questions." Click.

Darlene's problem appeared to be a language deficit because she used few words. However, language instruction did not help her. The reason is that her problem was even more basic: she could not remember a word because she had no mental image for what the word labeled. Her memory for specific objects in her environment was vague or nonexistent, and she could not name those objects. She needed to sharpen her images.

In a typical lesson, the teacher and Darlene mentally walked through a place that was very familiar, the neighborhood grocery store. "Let's think about the food in the grocery store," the teacher suggested. "Yep," Darlene replied, "food in the store." The teacher guided Darlene in this mental walk by giving her prompts and asking her clarifying questions as the following dialogue illustrates.

"Let's walk to the frozen foods section first, Darlene. Remember how cold that section is?" Darlene nods and smiles. "Yep," she replies, "makes my hands cold."

"What do you see there, Darlene?" the teacher asked. "Ice cream!" Darlene replied. The teacher guided Darlene to reach into the frozen food section and pull out a carton of ice cream. She then asked Darlene questions that helped her examine and clarify her image of ice cream.

"Tell me, Darlene," the teacher asked, "how does that carton feel in your hand? Oops, don't drop it! You know how slippery that carton can be! What does the carton look like?" the teacher asked. "Red and white,

and there's letters on it too," Darlene explained. "It's strawberry. I like strawberry. It's my favorite!" As Darlene examined and labeled her image with guidance from the teacher, language began to tumble out of her mouth. "And there's frosty stuff on the outside, slippery and cold, like glass!"

Darlene and the teacher moved on to the next task in the imaging process—drawing it. At first, Darlene could not draw pictures of her images, so the teacher drew them for her according to Darlene's directions. "Make a box!" Darlene directed her teacher. "What should I draw on the box, Darlene?" the teacher asked. "What do I need to put on here so that you'll think of ice cream?" Darlene thought a moment as she scanned her mental image. "Swirly things," she said, "that look like scoops of ice cream, and draw some letters on it too."

Working together in this fashion, Darlene and the teacher drew several grocery items. Darlene matched these picture note cards to corresponding word cards and read them. Darlene practiced by choosing a picture note card, saying its name, and then finding the word card to match.

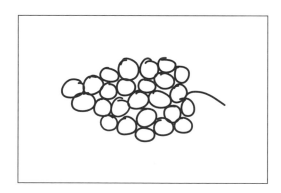

Darlene built clearer images of other less familiar words through similar dialogue and picture noting. She learned to notice details, clarify her images, and associate words to them herself. Note that the teacher did not need to teach her every word that she added to her vocabulary. Darlene learned how to build vocabulary on her own by noticing distinctive features and linking them to word labels.

The Imagery Base of Comprehension, *continued*

Eighteen-year-old Wilson is another case of ambiguous images and limited language. He used eight stereotypic phrases, and that was all he uttered. "Yah like big time wrestling?" he asked anyone who would listen. "I like big time wrestling! You like wrestling?" he asked again. Wilson had been educated as autistic, mentally retarded, and emotionally disturbed. He was a large healthy boy with an uneventful medical history except that his hearing was interrupted for two years from ages two to four.

Wilson's family believed that he had capabilities. He and his grandmother shared a paper route. One Sunday 125 changes were made in the paper route, and Wilson learned them all in one day. At the clinic he received a very superior score on a *Ravens Progressive Matrices Test*, a language-free exam. The teacher tried to teach him language, but Wilson's memory for word labels was fuzzy and elusive.

Wilson needed instruction in linking words to his images. He started learning with situations he knew well, such as the route to school. The teacher and Wilson laid out simple familiar scenes in three dimensions on a table while discussing and manipulating them. It was essential that Wilson move objects in the scene himself as he learned the language to label the objects. Wilson was able to understand objects directly without language. After all, he could deliver newspapers to houses. So manipulating objects first and then adding language labels allowed him to start his learning at a point where he was capable.

In one scene, a small box represented Wilson's house and a second box was a barn.

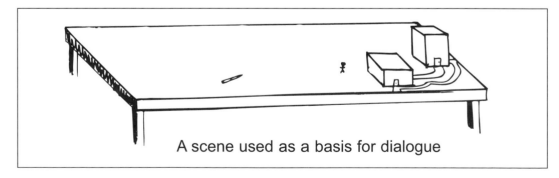

A scene used as a basis for dialogue

Teacher: *"Does your house have a door?"*
Wilson: *"Yep!"*

Teacher: (hands Wilson a pipe cleaner figure they made) *"Walk yourself to the barn."*
Wilson: (moves the figure)

The Imagery Base of Comprehension, *continued*

Teacher: *"Oh, you went out of the house door* (draws door) *and into another door on the barn* (draws barn door). *Is that in the right place?"*

Wilson: (looks at boxes) *"No, there."* (points to the end of the barn)

They redrew the door. Gradually the setting was expanded to include sidewalks, fields, bus stops, and the road to town. Wilson directed construction of the scene. The teacher and Wilson elaborated the language for each feature in his environment. His language grew.

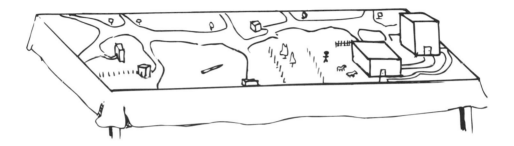

When the model was extensive and Wilson could describe it specifically, he was ready for the next step. He drew and labeled the scene in two dimensions, a more difficult task. Wilson took a long time to be ready to draw in two dimensions.

Through these exercises, the teacher put language into Wilson's world, a world that he had understood only directly through physical experience rather than through images and labels. He could not come to the teacher's way of knowing, so she brought language to his way of knowing the world.

Before long Wilson elaborated this new language for familiar places and began to attach language to many parts of his environment. His communication abilities expanded at a rapid rate.

Jacob, Darlene, and Wilson had problems with imaging. Jacob's and Darlene's images were ambiguous, so their word labels were elusive in memory. Imagine their difficulty remembering the word *maroon* when they did not precisely know maroon color and its difference from red or blue. Imagine trying to learn about the judiciary system when they could not picture what a judge does.

Wilson had an imaging problem too. He had some images in his memory that were apparently quite clear. For example, he knew exactly where to draw each of the doors on the boxes representing his family's farm buildings. He saw clearly in his mind each of the 125 new delivery points for his newspapers. However his labels for images were limited. He could not link images to oral or printed words. Thus, he spoke in stereotypic phrases often unrelated to the talk of others. As a result when asked, "How is school Wilson?" he might reply, "Do you like big-time wrestling?" In this way he was socially acknowledging the speaker.

Difficulties with imagery may be subtler than the cases of Jacob, Darlene, or Wilson. Symptoms of imaging problems may include forgetting important details, failing to grasp relationships such as comparative size or location, or losing track of directions or a story line. Some students fail to grasp what is read or heard especially when vocabulary becomes more difficult, such as in science or social studies textbooks. This problem usually becomes more evident in high school.

Students who do not read often have language deficits. However, as the above cases demonstrate, sometimes the problem is more fundamental than language—their images may be unclear or nonexistent. Like everyone else, Jacob, Darlene, and Wilson experience the world directly through the senses. However, unlike many people, they form images that are vague and elusive. As a result, they do not recapture the world with clarity, reliability, or specificity. Their ambiguous language represents their fuzzy imagery.

📖 Teaching How to Image

To help these people, the teacher must deal with the basic problem first—imaging. Constructing accurate images precedes attaching words to those images. Reading can then follow. The important point here is that imagery precedes language. If the student cannot image something, the language related to it will be vague or missing. The label also affects images in a reciprocal manner—language can clarify and specify images.

To help students who image poorly, teach them to make their images specific and to link language to their images. For example, you might have the student listen to a story, imagine that it's like a video playing, and draw a picture that captures the plot. (Review the Picture Notes section in Appendix 3, pages 143-144.) Later the student retells the story from this picture alone.

The Imagery Base of Comprehension, *continued*

For students who demonstrate severe difficulties with imagery, like Darlene or Wilson, a more strategic and comprehensive method of instruction is recommended. These students should practice imaging objects that are already familiar. With Darlene it was grocery store items, and with Wilson it was markers along the route to school. Often students can image life events more easily than print or conversation.

Strategies for Helping Individuals Overcome Imaging Problems

1. **Teach picture noting.** A picture note is a rapid sketch that captures the important characteristics of the object drawn. This drawing helps shape the student's memory. Accurate imaging is necessary for strong memory storage. However, even if a person images and stores information, he can still fail to retrieve a memory. Teaching students to image with picture notes addresses both storage and retrieval problems. Drawing pictures that capture the distinctive features of an object or an event clarifies the image and facilitates memory storage.

    Picture noting also creates a pathway for retrieving the item from memory. For example, linking a picture of a mailbox to the word allows one to access the word through the image of the mailbox, through the sound of the word, and through the appearance of the word, since all of these become associated in memory. Learning this linkage in a language-rich lesson results in multiple routes to memory retrieval.

    The student must be encouraged to control the construction of his own memory. He must create his own picture notes and other cues. Memory is not a template available in the same form to everyone. Whatever is stored in memory is individual and is constructed by each individual during storage and retrieval.

2. **Teach imaging objects.** Manipulating three-dimensional objects is the starting point for clarifying images. As the student examines the object, the teacher encourages him to describe it. To sharpen his visual images, the student also needs to draw picture notes, which illustrate unique features that define a word or idea. Talking about the object during this exercise attaches language to the student's world that was previously

known only vaguely or directly through the senses. In essence, the teacher meets the student in his sensory world and helps him label it with language.

Teacher: *"Take a look at this."* (hands student a stone with a fossil embedded in it)
Student: *"Gee, that feels good."*

Teacher: *"Smooth. What else do you notice about it?"*
Student: *"It's brown."*

Teacher: (removes rock) *"Did you recognize what that was?"*
Student: *"A snail?"*

Teacher: *"What do you suppose we call that?"*
Student: *"What's it called?"*

Teacher: *"Some people call these fossils."*
Student: *"Yeah, fossils."*

Teacher: *"What did you notice about the spiral shape?"*
Student: *"Curvy."*

Teacher: *"Did you notice colors?"*
Student: *"Brown, gray."*

Teacher: (teacher brings out the rock again) *"What do you notice now?"*
Student: *"Kind of pointy on top."*

Teacher: *"That's called a ridge. Some people might notice this little chunk. There are probably a lot of fossils shaped like this. Let's draw a note so that we will remember the rock whenever we see the note. Draw the features that make it unique.* (teacher and student each draw notes) *Tell me about your drawing."*
Student: *"It's a fossil...brown, a ridge, a spiral..."*

The student's ambiguous images become more clear and specific during this exercise.

The Imagery Base of Comprehension, *continued*

For more practice, the teacher can ask the student to bring items from home to put in a bag. The student describes each object in the bag as clearly as possible while the teacher makes a picture note. Then the student gets the object out of the bag and compares it to the teacher's note to see how clearly he described the object.

3. **Teach imaging pictures.** After practicing clear imaging with three-dimensional objects, a similar exercise provides practice in two dimensions. The teacher presents a slide or a picture very briefly and removes it.

> Teacher: *"Tell me what you saw."*
> Student: *"A person."*

> Teacher: *"What was the person doing?"*
> Student: *"Swinging something. There was blue behind."*

> Teacher: *"The person was swinging a golf club. What was blue?"*
> Student: *"The sky?"*

The teacher brings back the picture and asks the student to scan and clarify the image.

> Teacher: *"Now look at the picture again. What surprises you?"*
> Student: *"It's a woman. There is a..."*

> Teacher: *"Golf cart."*
> Student: *"Golf cart."*

> Teacher: *"What about the golfer makes her unique? Draw a picture note."*

From this practice with imagery and picture noting, the student learns the **process** of vocabulary building. He begins to notice independently the distinctive features of objects and pictures, and he applies specific language labels to these features and objects. His language and verbal memories grow and become clear.

Chapter 8: Language—Precursor to Reading

Difficulty with language is a common reason why people struggle with reading and writing. They must comprehend and use language before they can read it. In this chapter we discuss the impact of language on a student's academic progress and describe several ways to help students with language problems, including categorization for vocabulary development, scripting, and picture noting.

Age and Language

Language can be improved at any age and in any culture. Language is changeable throughout one's lifetime, not merely during the so-called critical period of youth. Also, blaming language deficits on peripheral issues such as poverty or culture clouds the responsibility to improve language. Humans are meant to learn language, and language deficits can and should be addressed.

The story of 40-year-old Lucille illustrates that language can be changed throughout one's lifetime. Lucille could neither read nor write, not even the names of her children. She had severe language processing problems that affected several aspects of her language system. She mixed up and ran words together. In fact, most people could not understand her at all! Lucille's problem was not mental retardation. Her job performance illustrated her intelligence. She planned and orchestrated food preparation for 300 people at a community center.

To teach Lucille, it was necessary to join her in **her** world and to build her minimal language system. Through this language instruction, Lucille learned to communicate orally and to read and write. She is now a leader in her community. People like Lucille challenge educators to their very limits and demonstrate that change is not only possible, but it should be expected.

The Language System

Language is a system comprised of reciprocal elements: receptive/expressive, reading/writing, and listening/speaking. These elements are interconnected in such a way that they interact and support each other in learning. To take advantage of these relationships, language should be presented as a whole system with each element taught with its reciprocal. Reading should be taught with writing and listening with speaking.

Like the listening/speaking and reading/writing reciprocals, language and thought are also connected. When language improves, thinking also changes. Lucille said she knew things that she was unable to put into language. Once she began to acquire language, her vocabulary started to burst. She said words that nobody knew she knew, including herself. Once she remarked, for example, "I'm beginning to think of a lot of words that I can now remember." Language allowed Lucille to access and use those words and those thoughts. Language also allowed her to evaluate events she previously had difficulty sorting out. As a member of the community center, for example, she refused to vote on a decision brought before the board. When asked why, Lucille explained, "I don't know enough to make a 'telligent decision!" Once her language improved, Lucille recognized not only what she knew, but also what she did not know.

Language and Behavior

Language affects other aspects of behavior. Sometimes children have behavior problems because they have language problems. They misbehave because they cannot manage their behavior with self-talk. *Self-talk* is verbal self-instruction that is overt in young children and internalized in adults. With difficult tasks, even adults direct themselves by talking out loud. Poor socialization can result when people are unable to use language appropriately to get along well with others, or they lack the ability to get their words out effectively and efficiently. Often they can end up in classes for the emotionally disturbed because they explode or withdraw when they are having strong emotions and do not have the language to express them.

Language Development: General to Specific

Language learned naturally develops from the general to the specific. For example, children learn words for dogs by starting with the general concept of dog and later differentiating between different types of dogs. Toddlers express broad ideas such as "Daddy go" before they perfect the specifics of words and grammar. Thus, language learning proceeds from the broad to the specific or from the top down. The toddler learning language does not put together sounds to make phonetic families of words and then build sentences from the bottom up. This understanding is important in the discussion of reading instruction.

📖 The Features of Language

Three basic features of language are syntax (grammar), semantics (vocabulary), and phonemes (sounds).

Syntax is the structure or grammar of language. It is the way that language is arranged according to rules about order. Lucille put language together randomly. Even her family did not understand her when she spoke to them on the phone. The reason is that she did not follow syntactic rules, which are clearly important to convey meaning. If language were just sounds and words thrown together, someone from a foreign country could get by with only a dictionary in a strange country. Clearly this does not work. Every language has a set of underlying rules about how to put it together in predictable patterns, and these rules of order are called syntax.

As structure develops, *semantics* or vocabulary is acquired. People cannot hold onto words without a structure to hang them on. So if a student demonstrates depressed vocabulary, instruction in syntax is often needed. Learning random words without an organizing structure is unnatural and difficult.

Phonemes are the sounds of language. Lucille left out certain sounds; she could not hear the difference between some sounds; and she could not say some sounds. She still could not pronounce some sounds even after she learned to read and write. A person like Lucille who has difficulty with sound discrimination or expression may confuse *velvet* with *valet* or *deaf* with *death*.

In spite of her language difficulty, Lucille did have important strengths to build on. She could understand both the syntax and the vocabulary of what she heard. The Language Features chart below shows that Lucille had receptive syntax and semantics channels open for learning.

Language Features	
Receptive Language	Expressive Language
Syntax (Grammar) Listening Reading	Syntax (Grammar) Speaking Writing
Semantics (Vocabulary) Listening Reading	Semantics (Vocabulary) Speaking Writing
Phonemes (Sounds) Listening Reading	Phonemes (Sounds) Speaking Writing

Language–Precursor to Reading, *continued*

📖 Analyzing Language Problems

Consider Mardell, a high school junior. Her grades in high school were declining. Before ninth grade, she received A's and B's and was considered a model student. Her hardest class in high school was biology, a course with difficult vocabulary. She also did not like civics because, as she said, "The teacher did not make any sense. He wandered all over the place, talking and talking." All the students in the class, except for Mardell, understood the history teacher quite well. She earned A's in English class where the emphasis was on writing and grades depended on the volume of writing produced. Mardell produced the required volume of writing. However, she was not a big talker. Her most frequent words were "um," "sorta," and "kinda."

Mardell had trouble with receptive vocabulary. Two clues were her dislike for chatting and for the wordy teacher. Another clue was her difficulty in subjects with high vocabulary demands, such as biology. She simply did not recognize the meaning of some words when she listened.

Mardell also had a problem with receptive syntax. She did not quickly process the structures that she heard. Mardell felt confused whenever she had to listen to a lot of complex language, such as a lecture from a civics teacher. The average person experiences similar confusion when listening to someone with an accent that interferes with listening comprehension.

Finally Mardell had trouble with speaking vocabulary because she could not retrieve words to express herself. Yet she could produce written vocabulary because she had more time to retrieve words while writing than while speaking.

Another example of language problems was nine-year-old Lisa. Lisa was the star of the classroom of children with behavior disorders. Either she acted very "prickly," or she would shut down communication and refuse to cooperate. If someone became insistent with her when she shut down, she would hit the person. Her speech consisted of a few stereotyped phrases delivered with great emphasis. Other features of her language disability were that she misunderstood a lot of what she was told, she never expressed her feelings, and she could not read or write. However, she had no problem understanding the sounds of words.

As indicated by her limited expressions, Lisa had problems with receptive and expressive syntax and vocabulary. Her acting out was additional evidence of language difficulties. When she could not understand or express herself with language, Lisa exploded or tuned out. Understanding and expressing feelings were very difficult for her. She could not differentiate between rage and elation in herself or others.

Another student, second-grader Kelly, could not read. Oh yes, he could recognize some individual words, decode a few sound sequences, and even read a minimal chunk of print here and there. However, he could not be considered a reader, and he seemed to be lagging further and further behind his peers in both reading and writing. He liked math and performed well on the math assignments in class, but whenever story problems were introduced, he did not know what was asked of him.

Kelly had been retained in first grade and was age appropriate for third grade. Since he was small for his age, he appeared to fit in physically with his second grade classmates. He seemed socially immature, striking other children in anger.

Initially, Kelly's problem appeared to be reading. However, he also had problems with speaking in terms of syntax, vocabulary, and sounds. Kelly swallowed words, which indicated that he did not hear or produce certain phonemes. He did a little better with receptive vocabulary and syntax. With language work, Kelly improved every area of language, including reading.

Kelly's word swallowing was a significant marker of articulation problems. Closer examination revealed that Kelly could not control his mouth movements. The longer the sentence, the more difficulty he had. Kelly could not sustain the motor sequences that speech requires. The inability to pronounce sentences profoundly affected other areas of Kelly's language. He needed an integrated speech, language, and reading program. However, reading was not the place to start instruction. He could not learn reading before language, before his listening comprehension approximated the language of print.

Language–Precursor to Reading, *continued*

📖 Strategies

The following strategies are suggested for addressing language problems.

1. **Teach categorizing.** If a student has trouble extracting the essential features of word meaning, instruction and rehearsal in categorization are helpful. Categorizing requires an examination and selection of features to use in sorting. For example, one can sort by categories like shape, color, size, or use.

   The junk box exercise provides opportunities to categorize. (See Appendix 4, pages 145-146.) The student sorts and sifts through a box full of items on a table and begins to group what goes together. The teacher encourages the student to talk during the process. A student might say, "That's not cloth...it's tall things that stand up...the balls go together...I suppose some things just don't fit into any pile."

   At first the teacher may need to help with categorization clues, "Okay, so this is the cloth or leather pile...this is the plastic pile...this is the paper pile." Then the student is usually able to classify the rest.

   The teacher and student discuss which feature to use for classification, noting that there is more than one possibility. Then the student may sort the objects again using different categories. The teacher and student should discuss why some things fit into a category and other things do not. This sorting process forces the student to identify essential features of items. This discussion allows a student to enrich and specify her word meanings.

   The junk box is an easy game that expands vocabulary and makes it more specific. It is a reminder that words are easier to learn in categories. Much of memory is arranged around categories of meaning. Learning lists of unrelated vocabulary words is unnecessarily difficult.

   A guessing game can also afford additional practice with specific features of words. One player describes an item according to its features, while the other guesses which item is being described. As the player identifies multiple features of objects, he expands and embellishes word meanings.

Language–Precursor to Reading, *continued*

2. **Teach picture noting.** In spite of learning vocabulary words, students may not be able to recall them when needed. Picture noting is a way to solve this problem. (See Appendix 3, pages 143-144.) It is a method to help students learn, retain, and recall words.

Picture notes are quick drawings that represent words or ideas. While drawing, the student must select distinctive features for the word or idea. Thus the drawing process clarifies words or ideas. Also the drawing is associated with the word or idea and triggers recall.

The following case illustrates using picture notes to clarify word meaning and trigger word recall. George had to learn the following 12 science vocabulary terms:

astronomical unit	meteoroid
stratosphere	nebular theory
core	prominence
corona	refracting telescope
meteor	solar system
meteorite	sunspot

Previously, he looked up definitions, memorized them, and failed the test. This time the teacher asked him to look up each word in the glossary or in the chapter where they appeared. As he looked up the words, he grouped them according to their meanings. This is the place where picture notes came in. George drew a picture of what his definition looked like for each word, distinguishing between similar words in a group. He grouped together *meteoroid*, *meteor*, and *meteorite* because they were similar and confusing to him.

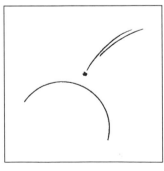
meteoroid

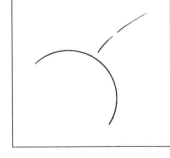
meteor

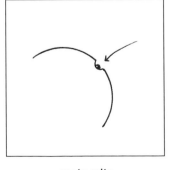
meteorite

George wrote word definitions containing clues to meaning. A meteor<u>oid</u> is out in the <u>void</u> (rhyming clue); a met<u>eor</u> enters the <u>earth</u>'s atmosphere, and a meteor<u>ite</u> b<u>ites</u> the earth. Note that George used his own words in these definitions just as he drew his own picture notes. The way images and words are stored in memory is individual, and students must store their own pictures and definitions.

George practiced going back and forth between word and picture notes, studying words in meaningful groups, and distinguishing carefully between the features of similar words. After this practice, he got 100% on the vocabulary test.

While a student with vocabulary difficulties is acquiring words, the teacher needs to accommodate instruction in the meantime so that the student will understand.

3. **Teach scripting.** A *script* is an established set of sentences or questions that helps a person execute a routine, such as getting ready for school, behaving correctly in a restaurant, or solving a math problem. For example, a script for leaving for school might go like this: "Coat, check backpack, lunch money, 7:15 out the door." This script directs behavior.

Students with language problems often have few or no scripts. Teaching them scripts directly helps them acquire control over their behavior. Without their own scripts, students need more directions from the teacher or the parent. A teacher talking to a student who lacks scripts might say, "Where is your pencil? Your paper? It's time to get started." The teacher or parent ends up managing the student's behavior. The adult's talk moves the student forward when she is stuck in a task sequence.

Scripts help a student manage behavior independently. Without scripts in her own language, she may do all right on homework, which can be done with notes and a textbook readily available. However, the student may be lost on closed book tests.

The following script example guides the student through division of fractions.

$$\frac{2}{3} \div \frac{1}{5} = \underline{\hspace{2cm}}$$

1. Invert the second fraction.

2. Multiply the top numbers together and then the bottom numbers together.

3. Reduce.

The script should be in the student's language, and the student needs to have an image for the action that accompanies each step. To teach a script, rehearse it with the student as she carries out the activity.

The student needs to keep the script within view while working. It can be written on a sticky note and attached close to the worksheet. It is useful to create a one-page summary of scripts about a topic, such as fractions, for quick reference and review.

To summarize, a script is a set of statements or questions that directs a person through a multi-step task. The task might be setting the table, feeding the dog, or solving division problems. People need scripts if they get stuck in a task and forget what to do next. Some individuals automatically formulate their own scripts, while other people, particularly persons with learning disabilities, need to be taught scripts. An effective script is written in a student's own words. It triggers the required actions and addresses the points where the student becomes stuck in the sequence of steps.

Language problems are discussed further in Chapter 9: Semantics, pages 91-97, and Chapter 10: Syntax, pages 98-102.

Chapter 9: Semantics

Vocabulary problems make academic subjects increasingly difficult as a student progresses in school and as textbooks get harder.

Consider the case of Mary, a high school student. Mary was her parents' great hope. They worked hard to save enough money to send her to college. Mary met her parents' expectations through junior high school, where she was a model student. She read without difficulty; in fact, she was phonetically skilled. On homework assignments and tests she could answer questions easily when the vocabulary for the answers was contained in the questions. However, when she had to construct answers with her own words, she had difficulty. In high school, her grades deteriorated from A's to C's and D's, especially in science and history.

What was she like outside of school? Mary's parents described her as a strong athlete but not much of a conversationalist. She said only "yes," "no," or "maybe" at the dinner table. Mary had friends, but she hated to talk on the phone, and she was not the one to initiate social events with peers.

Pam, a middle school student, also had word problems. Pam talked incessantly and communicated little. She drove her physician father crazy because her conversation lacked specificity. For example, she could not remember the right word for the item often seen hanging around her father's neck, a stethoscope. Pam would refer to it as, "You know, that thing around your neck; you know, what you use to listen to, oh yeah, the heart." For a pen, Pam might say, "You know what you call this; it's sort of a writing thing." Pam talked around words, focusing on function rather than on recalling the precise word. She performed poorly in discussions at school and was considered harebrained by her teachers and peers. However, Pam performed well when she wrote. In fact, she liked to write essays and research papers. Thus, teachers who evaluated students based on written performance thought Pam was doing well.

Lance, an elementary school student, had great difficulty learning the names for letters and words. He uttered few words and communicated little with anyone. He clung passively to adults, avoiding social contact with other children. If someone confronted him, he panicked. After repeating first grade, Lance was a non-reader. By this time he could sound out some words, but not consistently, and only those words that followed simple spelling patterns. Teachers tried to help by limiting the print to simple phonic patterns, but Lance did not advance with this help.

Students with depressed vocabulary are uncertain about the meaning of many of the words that are fundamental to school. They might copy the definitions of words verbatim or copy answers from the text verbatim, but they don't really understand.

Semantics, *continued*

Their lack of comprehension is evident on tests which require them to rephrase language rather than giving rote memorized responses. These students may resort to copying other people's answers. They may even plagiarize reports because they cannot state ideas in their own words.

In the above case, note that Mary's table talk was short on words. She also avoided the telephone which can be a sign of auditory processing problems or language deficits. A key clue is the point in school when Mary began to fail. Once she reached high school she could no longer read and get by, especially in subjects with high vocabulary demands. Probably the questions asked in these classes also required analytical answers with different vocabulary from the words in the questions. Mary could not express herself well in her own words. Overall, Mary's profile suggests that she had trouble with semantics.

Pam is a little different. She talked more than Mary, but notice the simple vocabulary in her speech. Perhaps she knew some words, but she had difficulty recalling specific word labels. She just could not come up with the precise word when she needed it. Pam's main problem was word finding or rapid verbal recall. Her writing was better than her speaking because she had time to reflect while writing. Poor word finding hindered her discussion in class. She also scored poorly on timed written tests that required many words.

Clearly, Lance lacked vocabulary knowledge. He neither understood nor expressed many words. Lance was a non-reader. Notice the social impact of semantic problems. Lance did not relate to his peers because he lacked the words to communicate with them. He panicked in confrontations because he lacked the words to defend himself or respond. Sometimes students who do not have the words to discuss their feelings erupt physically in frustration. Other times they just quit communicating and block people out. Lance needed language enrichment linked to semantic imagery.

Depressed vocabulary restricts a student's performance. It is hard to process and remember new knowledge without the necessary words. Students lacking words to express options often seem rigid in their views. The question the teacher needs to ask is, "How can I help students learn the concepts presented in class rather than memorize words and phrases which have little meaning to them?" These students need multiple alternatives: they benefit from both accommodations and from direct instruction in vocabulary.

Semantics, *continued*

📖 Accommodation Strategies

Students with vocabulary delays usually need an extensive amount of accommodation in a variety of ways. Here are some suggestions to consider.

1. **Preview vocabulary before a new lesson.** Students with semantics problems need an opportunity to learn background vocabulary for a lesson before the actual lesson is presented. Teachers should anticipate new words and teach them to the student before assigning reading.

2. **Provide modified texts.** Teachers can allow students to read easier books if the grade level text is too difficult. It is important to be aware of high vocabulary demands in subjects like science (especially biology), social studies, and literature. A good independent learner uses a variety of sources anyway. Asking the student to go to the library and find a better book or a video on the same subject enhances his independence as a learner. Sometimes teachers who do this find the student's choice of book better than their texts. It is important to give the student advance notice before a new unit begins so that he can find a book, learn vocabulary, and take any additional preparation steps.

3. **Provide supplementary materials.** Teachers can help by giving the student with vocabulary problems complementary materials such as an outline of a lesson or teacher lecture notes. The student can also use commercially available notes for specific topics or view a movie prior to reading a book. These extra materials give students the vocabulary context for classroom learning that other students likely already have.

4. **Select teachers carefully.** Sometimes students need to be matched with teachers who use language that is clear, simple, and comprehensible to them. Some teachers communicate with complex vocabulary or with scattered and disjointed language, confusing a student who has limited vocabulary.

Semantics, *continued*

5. **Accept the student's vocabulary.** Teachers should allow students to express themselves in their own way rather than require them to use vocabulary beyond their level. Students may be responding with the correct meaning even though they may not use just the right word. Flexibility and support by the teacher are helpful. Students should be allowed to rewrite test questions in their own words so that they can understand and respond.

6. **Avoid rote work.** Schoolwork calling for rote responses does not help students develop comprehension. Rote is copying the meaning of a word out of the dictionary and memorizing it. Rote is answering noninferential questions by copying sentences from the book. It is also studying poetry by memorizing a poem. Instead, students need to reflect and express their own ideas in words that do not appear on a page before them. Anything less encourages mindless copying, not comprehension.

7. **Use visual cues during instruction.** The teacher should use pictures, diagrams, drawings, or demonstrations during class presentations to illustrate ideas. Visual cues help when vocabulary is limited.

8. **Provide alternative instructional approaches.** Students should be allowed to use learning resources other than text, such as video, peer cooperative learning groups, interviews with experts, or real experiences in the school or community. However, the teacher needs to allow time to prepare these activities and to be careful about extra work for a student with delayed vocabulary.

9. **Encourage use of a thesaurus.** A thesaurus in a word processor is an excellent asset for students who have problems finding the right word.

Instructional Strategies

For the student with severe deficits in semantics, vocabulary instruction is essential. This instruction should be multisensory, experiencing words through hearing, reading, and writing. Specifically, the student can use visual notes, real experience with semantic content, or webbing. The latter is the study of words in meaningful groups.

1. **Teach picture notes.** (See Appendix 3, pages 143-144.) Relating visual images to a word label improves memory for the word, especially when images evoke both the meaning of the word and the sound of the label. With this approach, the student increases the recall routes to the word in his memory, creating links between the sound of the word, a visual image of the word, and the meaning of the word.

   The student draws a picture on a note card that cues the meaning of the vocabulary word and usually another picture that cues the sound of the word. Sometimes the same picture cues both the sound and the meaning. The meaning picture must capture the essence of the word's meaning—the distinctive features of the word. After all, ambiguity of understanding is often a reason why the word is not remembered. Here are some examples.

   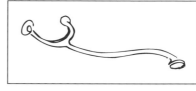

   To remember the word *stethoscope*, the student draws a stethoscope to trigger the meaning of the word. To trigger the label, the student might draw a microscope along with a picture of a tongue because pronouncing the word *stethoscope* requires some odd tongue action.

   Understandably, the hardest words to remember are abstract ones like *democracy*. The harder an abstract word is, the more difficult and the more important it is for the student to grasp its meaning. Hence, even with abstract words, the student must extract the essence of the word's meaning and draw it. For *democracy*, the student might draw many people and a government building to relate the word to its essential meaning. Visual notes are individual. Students make up and draw their own with the teacher's guidance.

   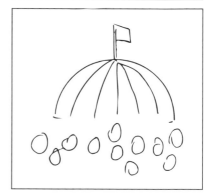

2. **Teach through real experience.** Memory for vocabulary works better when it is linked to real experiences. Students can encounter meaning "hands on" or relate the word to an experience they have already had. Direct experience is multisensory and builds enriched associations. Enhancing associations to a word increases the ways that it can be recalled.

Semantics, *continued*

A challenge with experiential learning is translating and interpreting the three-dimensional world to the two-dimensional world of print. Some people may know a mango in the three-dimensional world, for example, but have trouble understanding the picture or printed word on a two-dimensional page. We discuss this issue in more detail in Chapter 15: Spatial Relations, pages 117-126. The point should be made here, however, that some people with spatial problems also have difficulty learning vocabulary because even though they recognize three-dimensional images easily, they don't recognize those images in print.

One solution to the problem of dimensions is that visual cues to vocabulary can be in the three-dimensional world rather than just on two-dimensional paper. For example, three-dimensional models can be used to teach body parts in biology. Medical students sometimes put on plastic suits and draw the nervous system on each other. Physical interaction with the real world enhances vocabulary learning because it builds multisensory associations with words. The student hears, sees, manipulates, and says the word. Remembering the word for *stethoscope* is much easier when experiencing a real example with all of the senses rather than just coming across the word in print.

3. **Teach categorizing.** It is helpful to present words in meaningful groups rather than in lists of unrelated items, such as 10 random words that begin with the letter "a." We learn vocabulary naturally in word families related to a particular experience or place, such as the theater, shopping mall, or beach. We also learn to describe details of meaning by comparing words in groups, such as contrasting types of cars or holds in wrestling. Group words in meaningful stories, functions, or routines. *Routines* are sequences of behavior expected in common situations or locations, such as in a restaurant (sit/order/eat/pay), at a ticket window (wait in line/buy ticket/go in), or at a school locker (open lock/put in items/take out books/close locker/lock it).

4. **Teach webbing.** A visual display of how one word relates to the other is called *webbing*. Seeing and discussing a visual diagram of related words enhances comprehension and memory and distinguishes between related words. The following web illustrates different meanings for *party*.

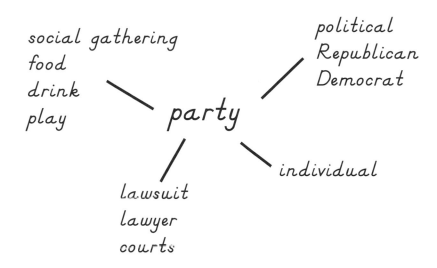

Another type of webbing exercise is to think of all the words that mean *anger*, put them on some sort of continuum, and compare them.

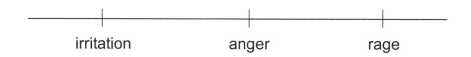

irritation   anger   rage

In summary, the teacher should prioritize word study according to the student's most immediate needs. In the previous examples, Lance needed labels for his feelings in order to express his frustrations and deal with his emotions. Mary needed vocabulary study for her immediate science and history problems.

For students with severe language delays that involve sentence structure as well as vocabulary, the teacher might use the ideas in Chapter 10: Syntax, pages 98-102. Sentence Builders/Word Shapes is a useful set of materials that allows the student to learn sentence patterns by physically manipulating geometric shapes that represent parts of speech. (See Appendix 2, pages 136-142.)

Chapter 10: Syntax

Syntax is the structure of language which is governed by rules of word order and grammatical forms. Syntactic patterns provide a framework in which words can be varied to produce an infinite variety of utterances. For example, the sentence "David plays outside" has a basic pattern of actor-action-adverb. New sentences can be generated by substituting different words into this pattern: "Mary plays outside." "Mary plays happily." "Janet sings happily." All of these sentences have the same pattern.

People who have syntactic deficits lack the fluent use of language pattern. They also fail to find meaning in the relationship between words in sentences and in word order. ("Does he play?" versus "He does play.") They miss inferential meaning, which comes from relating words and projecting understanding beyond the literal page.

Consider Frank, age 30, who was stuck at the second grade reading level. He could not spell. He spoke and wrote in simple sentences, using only chronological order as a structure: "I got up. I ate. I mowed the lawn." Frank dropped out of high school, never having learned to read. He got by because he was in special education classes and because he was intelligent.

During Frank's adult years, other people did not know about his reading deficits because he hid them successfully. In fact, he worked hard to do so. Even his wife did not know that Frank read very little. He faked reading common items like the newspaper.

Frank lacked the analysis skills typical of good readers, such as the ability to compare, comment, contrast, or any other process requiring the relation of ideas. Instead, he rigidly communicated in very simple sentences and structured his language in chronological order.

In contrast to his simple language, Frank could do complex, creative work with his hands. He remodeled his whole kitchen. He learned on the job how to completely wire a house. He could decipher the complex diagrams in an electrical manual. However, he failed the state electrician's test because of his reading difficulty.

Mandy, a third grader, did not like to read. She could not spell or read very many words, and she usually said she was tired while reading. When her teacher asked her to describe what she just read, she could not answer. Mandy did not read aloud well, and she did not read with the type of inflection that demonstrates sentence understanding. She read mechanically, word by word. Without strong external cues, Mandy did not read past the first grade level. Mandy really wanted to do well. She turned red and almost cried during reading class. She hid her reading book in frustration.

First grader Joe was not reading. In contrast to his family members who spoke accurately, he made grammatical errors in his speech such as "he runned away" and "I gots a dime." He had articulation problems also. Joe had an average vocabulary, was a good speller, and was bright and energetic, but he expressed himself in simple sentence fragments. When he was asked to dictate a sentence or two about a picture, he used incomplete sentences and nonspecific words. He watched wrestling with his dad and could recite all the wrestlers' names and the holds.

These cases illustrate reading problems that occur along with poor syntax. When students can read in first grade and then have difficulty at about second grade, syntax is often the problem because syntax becomes complex at this point in reading texts. This is also the point when pictures usually no longer predict the print on the page.

Even though Frank could read chunks of print and diagrams from the electrician's handbook because he knew the material from experience, he could not understand the electrician's exam questions because of the syntactic requirements of the task. Answering questions involves reversing word order while going from question to answer. He could not match the question language on the electrician's test to the language in his book and in his memory because the syntax was different.

Mandy read text as though it was a list of unconnected words. Also, she could not answer comprehension questions. She lacked the syntax to relate words and make meaning, which is a basic process in reading comprehension.

Joe's oral language did not approximate the sentence patterns of written language. The evidence is obvious in his grammatical errors: "He runned away," and "I gots a dime." Joe could not produce the syntax found in early readers. Clearly he was intellectually capable because he had an average vocabulary, could follow directions, and could relate details about any wrestling match that he had ever seen.

Sometimes syntax problems are apparent by a student's overly simple sentences or grammatical errors. People with syntax problems may progress to higher grades or to the work world because they are persistent, quiet, and guarded about their reading problems like Frank.

Sometimes the problem only becomes apparent on tests. High scores in word identification (decoding) along with low scores in reading comprehension point to syntax deficits. Another obvious marker of syntax problems is low scores on grammar tests.

📖 Strategies

1. **Teach syntax physically.** People with syntax deficits need to learn the patterns of language. The Sentence Builders/Word Shapes* give the student a visual representation of syntax and allow her to manipulate sentence patterns physically. (See Appendix 2, pages 136-142.) These materials allow for a multisensory approach. The student hears, manipulates, says, reads, and writes syntactic patterns. Each grammatical element, such as a verb or an adjective, is represented by a color-coded plastic shape. The student learns to represent the various types of sentences with a sequence of shapes, such as simple sentences and those with relative clauses. By using the shapes to construct patterns, building first one type of sentence and then another, the student can actually see syntactic rules at work, such as reversing subject and verb to form a question. Sentence Builders/Word Shapes is a logical starting point because it allows the student to work in the three-dimensional world, which is easier than two-dimensional print.

2. **Practice sentence combining.** The teacher can use a variety of ways to get the student to form and practice more complex sentences. To cue a compound sentence, the teacher can ask for two sentences about a picture. Then the teacher and student can explore ways to combine the two ideas into a compound sentence. To elicit a relative or subordinate clause pattern, the teacher needs to ask for two sentences about one thing in the picture. The student can dictate her combination sentence to the teacher, who then writes the sentence on adding machine tape and cuts and moves sections around to demonstrate variation of sentence patterns. Here are some examples of complex sentence exercises.

   The frog is sitting on the lily pad.
   The frog is catching a fly on its tongue.
   becomes
   The frog that is sitting on the lily pad is catching a fly on its tongue.

   The snow fell all morning.
   Our truck got stuck.
   becomes
   Because the snow fell all morning, our truck got stuck.

*Available from the Ark Foundation, Allenmore Medical Center, Suite A311, 1901 South Union, Tacoma, WA 98405, (253) 573-0311

The student must discover the relationship between the two ideas in order to form the complex sentence. The relationship might be one of time or cause and effect.

3. **Teach identification of complex sentences.** Once the student can do the exercises on the previous page with a minimum of external cues, she should move on to identifying the different types of sentences in text. Then she can ask questions of the print that elicit the various syntactic relationships such as a "when" question to elicit an "after" clause. This type of practice is also part of Sentence Builders/Word Shapes except that doing it with actual print rather than in a highly structured exercise is the next more difficult step.

4. **Cue pattern practice.** The teacher can provide visual word cues for pattern practice such as the *who*, *which*, and *that* below. The student fills in the blanks in many ways, creating a variety of sentences with the same syntax.

Mandy, who likes popcorn, ate the whole bagful.

_____, who _____ , _____.

_____, which _____ , _____.

_____, that _____ , _____.

Before she swept the walk, Nicole did the dishes.

After _____, _____.

Before _____ , _____.

Nicole did dishes after she swept the walk.

_____ after _____.

_____ before _____.

Here is a dialogue involving pattern practice with the conjunction *after*.

Teacher: *"I will eat lunch after you bake bread."*
Teacher: *"wash dishes"*
Student: *"I will eat lunch after you wash dishes."*

Teacher: *"finish the homework"*
Student: *"I will eat lunch after you finish the homework."*

Teacher: *"I will scrub the floor."*
Student: *"I will scrub the floor after you finish the homework."*

After practice with individual sentences, the teacher can ask the student to dictate her own paragraphs that include these patterns.

5. **Rehearse writing complex patterns.** Once students can identify the distinctive features of a pattern and produce it orally, they must learn to write it. This will follow naturally because students with syntax deficits may be able to write words quite well. They start by dictating their sentences to the teacher, who types them. Once they can read back their own typed sentences, they are ready to read the complex language of other writers.

   While writing these sentences, the teacher should ask for active writing patterns such as "she gardens" rather than "she is in the garden." This keeps written language more active and specific.

6. **Teach stopping language.** When working with complex syntax, one can lose the main point in the complexity of the language. Therefore, the student needs to practice deciding which is the dependent clause, which is the independent clause, and what is the central meaning. When working with convoluted language, the student needs to stop occasionally and find the main point, the actor, and action. We call this "stopping language."

Chapter 11: Attention—A Prerequisite to Learning

Inattention has a direct effect on reading. Students must attend in order to learn. Attention is necessary to notice what makes a "d" different from a "b" or to select the sound features that make a "scream" different from a "stream." Attention involves listening for the meaning of the whole stimulus as well as screening out irrelevant information, such as the squeaky pencil sharpener, the sounds outside the window, and the movement in the hallway. Attention is needed to remember to do an assignment and also to turn it in.

Attention problems occur in many forms. Consider the following cases.

Trisha was falling behind in reading in the third grade. She was usually slow to get started with anything, and she was often late for school because she had trouble getting up in the morning. During class she frequently wandered to the pencil sharpener, gazed out the window, and even fell off her chair. Her eyes followed the teacher as he explained how to do the assignment. Her hand did not move when he asked if anyone had a question. She listened but did not hear, and she did the wrong assignment. Aside from her low energy level, Trisha seemed competent and unremarkable in her skills and in her interactions with others. In fact, her problems often went unnoticed because she was quiet in class.

Jake, a junior in high school, usually fell asleep in his English literature class. He was passing all of his other classes, and he was doing excellent work in math and physical education. However, he accomplished very little in English.

Mark was physically very active in his special class in seventh grade reading. He responded well in discussion and seemed awake and energetic. However, his achievement in reading was not improving. A closer look revealed that Mark attended to the first few minutes of reading and then his energy turned elsewhere; he looked around the class, walked around, or talked to his classmates.

Mark's mother recently came to school to discuss problems she was having with him at home. She said that he did not think about the consequences of his actions. Sometimes his behavior seemed reckless, such as leaving the faucets on at home. His mother explained to him why he should turn the faucets off, but ten minutes later he turned on two faucets and forgot about them. Mark's mother then complained about his carelessness. Once he picked up a container of fifty sewing needles and, in spite of his mother's warnings, dropped them all on a thick pile rug! His mother also said that Mark was constantly losing his possessions. A typical after school conversation with him went something like this: "Where are your glasses?" "Oh...I had them in school." "Where is that blue shirt that I gave you?" "Somebody took it...I think."

All of these students have attention problems. However, each one represents a different kind of attention problem that teachers meet in schools from time to time.

Trisha had difficulty with attention activation. She had trouble getting her motor running to get up in the morning or to get started on her work in school. She may have had a physical health problem, depression, or Attention Deficit Hyperactivity Disorder (ADHD). Note that ADHD occurs in a variety of types and looks different in different people. The major symptoms are inattention, impulsivity, and hyper-activity/restlessness. However, individuals may not have all of these symptoms. A psychologist and/or a doctor with expertise in ADHD should evaluate a student like Trisha.

Jake was selective about his inattentiveness. He avoided English because he did not like the class. He did not have learning or attention problems.

In many areas of his life, Mark had a very brief attention span. He was easily distracted at school and at home. His impulsiveness and lack of vigilance indicate possible ADHD. This child needs assessment by a psychologist or a physician.

ADHD undermines effective reading. Without strong focus, a beginning reader may not look at words carefully enough to read and spell words accurately. The student may have the ability to analyze what is important in a paragraph, but he does not maintain attention and manage his reading analysis. In class he reacts impulsively without thinking; he does not analyze before blurting out the answer to a question.

Strategies

1. **Consider health factors.** Teachers and parents need to know that sometimes health factors such as allergies, ear infections, or chronic illness impede attention. These health problems need to be addressed before the student can learn comfortably.

    Some students tune out from time to time and miss items in clusters. This may be a sign of a neurological problem like petit mal, or they may have hormonal problems that reduce their energy levels. They may have ADHD and would benefit from appropriate medication. Those who are hearing impaired lack the external auditory cues that can help them attend. The physical problem may be lack of exercise, and daily activity might help. Inattention and lack of focus can also be signs of depression. Trisha's lack of energy could indicate depression.

2. **Assign reading at the student's ability level.** In order for a student to attend well, he must be capable of doing the work. An inattentive student may not be ready for the reading tasks before him. Learning disability in reading or language can look like an attention problem when a student does not attend because he cannot perform.

3. **Provide external cues.** The teacher may be presenting difficult material too soon without sufficient external cues. Students lose focus when the teacher progresses too fast. An example would be presenting new vocabulary to second graders and immediately thereafter giving them a homework assignment to write a paragraph using the words. Students often need more external cues from the teacher before they can work with new material independently. The teacher must cue the students appropriately as they progress through increasingly more difficult activities like the following.

   • Recognize new words.
   • Use the words in structured exercises.
   • Use the words in an original paragraph in a homework assignment without direct teacher support.

4. **Examine tracking demands and the student's ability to track.** The student could have a problem tracking with his eyes what he is reading. This could be a physical problem or just immature efforts toward self-control. The teacher could show the student how to track the material as he reads by moving his finger across the page or by holding a card under the line being read.

   One should note that tracking from the board to a desk can be difficult for some young children. If so, the teacher can use handouts instead of the board because tracking from page to page on a desk is usually easier.

5. **Build student awareness of attention problems.** The student may not attend to the task because he is unaware of his distraction. The teacher can work with the student to help him notice his inattentiveness. The first step is for the teacher and student to agree on the troublesome behaviors, such as wandering about the classroom or looking out the window. The second step is to design a way to look at those behaviors at specific and regular intervals throughout the day.

One highly effective way is for the teacher and the student to construct a rating sheet. Then they meet during brief but regular intervals to rate the behaviors in question, compare their perceptions, establish a dialogue, and plan for the next chunk of time. (See Chapter 4: Self-Management of Reading, pages 47-56.)

6. **Establish a purpose.** Students should be encouraged to develop personal reasons for reading their assignments. However, at times, they may read simply to pass a course. Teachers and students should accept individual differences in motivation and verbalize them.

7. **Limit the amount of reading.** Agree with students not to read beyond a certain point, thus limiting the amount of reading. Students with attention problems need to feel that their task is finite and that the end is reachable. They will probably learn to cue themselves internally to set reasonable limited goals if the teacher allows them to have a say in how much to read.

8. **Teach scripts.** A *script* is the set of questions or directions each person uses to guide his own attention through a task. If students do not use their own internal scripts to talk themselves through a task, the teacher can teach them scripts directly. Generating and asking questions is an effective study technique. For example, students can maintain focus on reading a chapter with questions such as:

   • What is going on in this chapter?

   • What is the main idea?

   • Look at the titles and the pictures and tell how the chapter is organized or divided. What questions does each section answer?

   • What are the answers to those questions?

   Students are encouraged to construct script questions in their own words. They keep these questions handy for whenever they read a chapter. They tape the script to their desk, keep it as a bookmark, or save it in their wallets.

Here is an example of a student's thoughts while reading a chapter with his script.

Q. What is the main idea?
A. Rome.

Q. How is this chapter divided?
A. I'll take a look at the subtitles. One chunk might be government, another what the people did every day, another the classes of people, and another artist contributions.

Q. Now I need a question for each section. For the first section, I could ask what kind of government they had.

Scripts are also very useful for directing attention to a task at home. Faced with a complex task like cleaning a room, a child might use a script to direct attention to getting started and following each step to completion. The script might go like this:

- Pick up everything and put it away.

- Put the garbage in the basket.

- Put the dirty clothes in the hamper.

- Vacuum the floor.

A parent can teach the child by modeling the steps while saying the script. Or the child can write the script in his own words or draw picture notes to use as a guide when he cleans the room. The script should be posted in an appropriate place in the home.

9. **Provide predictability.** Students with diffuse attention usually benefit from a structured learning environment. They tend to work better with a predictable teacher than with a disorganized one. These students usually like to anticipate a regular daily schedule. They need to be told in advance that a test or a field trip is scheduled. If they cannot remember a schedule, they may ask the teacher repeatedly what will happen next. Writing the schedule for the day helps solve this problem.

10. **Refocus attention.** The teacher should anticipate points in a lesson where focus will drop and plan for activities that refocus attention. Readers can regain control of attention by summarizing, finding main ideas, and drawing picture notes. Also, individuals have different attention spans, which can be known and dealt with directly. If Mark and his teacher know that he loses focus every ten minutes, Mark needs to recognize the length of his attention span and take a break before he loses focus. For example, if his attention span is ten minutes, he should take a break regularly—about every ten minutes. Effective break activities might include walking, getting a drink, stretching, or flexing muscles. Physical movement helps refocus attention.

    Once the student understands the nature of his attention span, he can be taught to ask for what he needs such as a schedule for the day, known limits on the amount of reading, a set of script questions for a new task, or a periodic break.

    Attention problems and resulting off-task behavior discourage teachers and parents. Mark could not sit down and his teacher disliked how he behaved. The two of them worked together on designing a plan to change behavior. They listed the troublesome behaviors and chose a couple of them to work on at a time. They met regularly to rate his behaviors, and, in this process, the teacher's behavior became more supportive as well.

Chapter 12: Auditory Discrimination & Memory

Students with reading and spelling problems may not be able to distinguish specific auditory differences. Reading instruction built on "sounding out" is extremely difficult for students who cannot discriminate similar sounds. They may need visually based instruction. Once visual patterns are known, they may be able to use this information to differentiate sounds.

Sam could not discriminate sounds in words accurately. The rest of his first grade class had learned all of the letters of the alphabet and their sounds. Sam, however, knew only letter names. He rattled off "a, b, c, d," but he could not consistently remember the sounds of the letters. His vocabulary was above average, although he made some pronunciation errors. All of his intelligence and language test scores were average except word discrimination, which required him to listen to two similar words and tell whether they were the same or different. He could not do this consistently.

Martha was having difficulty reading and spelling in fourth grade. She heard a spelling word as a blur of sound, omitted whole syllables in words, and mixed up letter order. She wrote *pre* for *per*, *shcool* for *school* and *nessary* for *necessary*.

Auditory problems may take on several forms even in children who have normal hearing thresholds such as Sam and Martha.

1. Students may not notice differences between similar sounding words such as *bread* and *bed* or *sit* and *sat*.

2. Students may not distinguish beginning sounds such as those in *pear* and *bear* or *please* and *fleas*.

3. Students may not discriminate different ending sounds such as those in *deaf* and *death*.

4. Students may not be able to differentiate meanings of words with similar sound patterns substituting *solitary* for *solidarity*, *hedges* for *hinges*, or *scheme* for *scan*.

5. Students may not differentiate rhyming words such as *gaunt* and *haunt* and may use one in place of the other.

In addition to distinguishing sounds in words, there is also the problem of segmenting words into sounds. For example, some people like Martha cannot segment a word like *grill* into component sounds in the correct order. They do not hear the difference between *gri* and *gir*. As a result, they may hear and even see *grill* and confuse it with *girl*. They may read and write *grill* and *girl* interchangeably.

Auditory Discrimination & Memory, *continued*

Word segmentation is the ability to divide a word into its component sounds in sequence: *sift* is s - i - f - t. It is also the ability to generate the word *sift* by cueing each letter in the word with its sound: the sound /s/ cues the letter "s," next the sound /i/ cues the letter "i," and so on. People with word segmentation problems may omit whole syllables and write *rember* for *remember*.

📖 Strategies

1. **Obtain a hearing examination.** Always start with the obvious. People with auditory discrimination problems may have hearing problems, and they should have their hearing evaluated. Sound discrimination problems can result from ear or adenoid infections, especially during the early childhood period of normal language learning. A hearing aid might be needed. However, people can hear and still be unable to discriminate differences between some speech sounds.

2. **Consider speech factors.** Students with auditory problems may have speech impediments as well. These students need a combination program incorporating language, speech, and reading instruction. Refer the student to a speech and language specialist to assist with this program.

3. **Combine motor and picture clues.** To learn the sound and symbol for "t," show the student how to touch the tip of her tongue to the roof of her mouth when pronouncing "t." Then encourage the student to draw a tongue tip out of the written letter "t." This picture note will remind the student of the sound of "t."

4. **Practice discriminating similar sounds.** See Chapter 1: Basic Reading, pages 9-27, to practice /a/ versus /e/.

5. **Teach visual phonics.** (See Chapter 1: Basic Reading, pages 9-27.) A person with auditory discrimination problems may benefit from visual opportunities to learn, perhaps throughout life. The multisensory approach suggested here allows the student to learn visually, thereby compensating for auditory weakness.

Chapter 13: Visual Discrimination & Memory

Most readers see a word or a letter pattern once and know it. They rely on their visual memories to read and spell similar letters like "d" and "b" or "ch" and "sh." They remember to write *seek* rather than *seak*, and they easily recognize visually distinctive words like *apple*.

However, some readers cannot discriminate specific visual differences in letters, numerals, and words. As a result their memories are imprecise and inadequate to trigger recall when they encounter a word in print or try to write the word.

Reading is both a visual and an auditory task. If visual input is inaccurate, the decoding process remains labored and tedious. Furthermore, the student is disadvantaged when reading the many words that are not phonetically based, such as *once*, *neighbor*, and *foreign*. Students with visual memory problems will tend to spell phonetically, even when inappropriate, since they are unable to recall visual differences and depend on sound differences. They may spell *machine* as *masheen* and *people* as *pepul*.

Sandy, a fourth grader, did not name all of her letters accurately and she misread most words. If she learned a word that was difficult for her, Sandy forgot it by the next day. If she learned a letter and the type of print was changed significantly, Sandy would not recognize the letter. Often when she wrote a letter, she formed it a new way, frequently checking the letter chart on the classroom wall. Even after this checking, she often wrote letters incorrectly. Sandy discriminated between sounds which she heard very well, and she demonstrated no other discernible problems.

Sandy attended a special education classroom for three hours a day where the teacher helped her finish her work for the regular class. Her mother also helped Sandy with homework each night for several hours. However, it was nearly impossible to complete written work and to write fourth grade essays because Sandy struggled with reading and writing individual letters and simple words. Schoolwork overwhelmed her.

Sandy's problem was visual. She could hear differences between sounds, but she did not learn the visual symbols accurately. Sandy did not recognize the distinctive features of letters and remember them. She did not know what features were essential to a "b" that discriminated it from a "d."

Austin was a 26-year-old high school graduate. He could read newspapers and magazines if he already knew about the content or if the print had many picture clues. However, he made many reading errors. He even got lost while driving because he misread street signs.

He worked his way up in a warehouse and had an opportunity to become foreman. However, he could not read his orders or fill out reports. When Austin tried to read his order forms, he would read *2100* for *1200*, *grass* for *gross*, and *carload* for *carton*.

Austin tried coping with the job requirements by taking the entire written work home for his wife to complete, but she soon tired of the drudgery. When someone asked him to read at work, Austin panicked. One day his boss came to him with reports that Austin had not completed. He told Austin that if he could not keep up, he would lose his job. Even though Austin organized people well and production had gone up under his leadership, he would have to leave.

Austin could read only with strong contextual support from which he guessed as he read. His problem was with individual words in isolation. From the evidence, he made visual errors, mistaking words that were slightly similar with the same initial letter and somewhat the same meaning. *Carton* and *carload* are similar, and both mean an amount. He would expect a word for amount and might choose the wrong one. In the context of his job, such an error could be very important.

📖 Strategies

Many methods have been described in other chapters and in the appendices to help people with visual discrimination and visual memory problems such as Sandy and Austin. The following list summarizes instructional approaches and refers to detailed descriptions elsewhere in this book.

1. **Teach symbol stabilization.** The purpose of symbol stabilization is to clarify and strengthen a student's visual memory for letters, words, and numerals. (See Appendix 1, pages 129-135.)

2. **Teach picture noting.** Drawing an image or idea to be remembered helps explicate and reinforce memory. Visual memory is highly individual. Picture notes require the student to make personal visual links that allow for this individualization. (See Chapter 7: The Imagery Base of Comprehension, pages 73-81, and Appendix 3, pages 143-144.)

3. **Teach spelling strategies.** Because so many English words include silent letters or variations of pronunciation, good spellers need more than phonic skills. They use visual memory to recall the appearance of words. A poor speller usually needs to learn strategies to improve his visual memory for words. (See Chapter 2: Spelling—A Skill Linked to Reading, pages 28-36.)

4. **Discuss language features.** Talking about a word will often highlight features of the word sufficiently to allow accurate recall. This is especially true if the student has auditory strengths. Making stories about the word personalizes details, which in turn strengthens successful recall.

5. **Use motor memory.** Students who have strong fine motor skills may remember words by writing them several times. Memory for the movement involved in writing reinforces visual differences for the image of the word. This strategy is not helpful for students who lack strong fine motor skill.

6. **Use three-dimensional letter activities.** Plastic letters such as those in the Symbol Stabilization exercises can be used in various ways beyond those already suggested. One example involves looking at a troublesome word and holding it in memory while walking across the room to a tray of letters to select the letters and make the word. At first, students tend to need reinforcing peeks back at the word, but they can increase their skill at retaining the word in memory with practice. (See Chapter 1: Basic Reading, pages 9-27, and Appendix 1, pages 129-135.)

7. **Use spaced practice.** A teacher or parent can help young students solidify word memory by asking for a spelling written in the air or on paper at spaced intervals throughout the day. This rehearsal strategy is useful for the occasional word family pattern or monster word that is hard to retain.

Chapter 14: Sense of Direction

Lindy, a third grader, mixed up *was* and *saw*, *b* and *d*, *u* and *n*, and *h* and *y* when she read and when she wrote. She wrote some symbols, like "3," backwards much of the time, and she reversed two digit numbers, reading "21" as "12." She frequently put her heading in the wrong corner of her worksheet. Sometimes she was confused about the direction in which to write. Also, she could not read a simple map to get somewhere like the rest of her classmates.

Lindy demonstrated many aspects of directional confusion, both left/right ("b" and "d") and up/down ("h" and "y"). She was confused about the direction of symbols and words that are the same except for their orientation in space. She was also confused about which way to move physically when writing, dancing, or playing games.

Directional orientation is a distinctive feature of many letters. Since direction is a spatial component of reading, this unit could be included in the chapter on spatial relations. It is separated out for special attention because the problem is so common and important in reading and writing disorders.

Directional problems can go undetected. The errors are not always pervasive. They can occur only in a student's writing or only in her reading. Some students learn to compensate with verbal scripts or other devices. Teachers need to be watchful to detect the problem.

Lindy needed to orient herself in a manner that was always available to her. Right and left, north and south did not work. Anchoring to the writing hand did not work. Lindy was right-handed, but she did not "feel" her handedness. However, placing a thick ruler on the left side of the desk allowed Lindy to "feel" the uniqueness of left versus right. This only worked if she gripped the ruler with her left hand to "know" that side as different from the right hand.

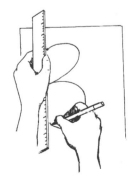

Body involvement also helped her learn the direction of numbers. For "3" she said, "I'm sitting on the ruler. Now I swing up and around in a big curve until I come back and kiss the ruler. Then I do it again and stop." When she used this script, she could write 3 accurately unless she was tired and forgot to use her cue. She also could go back and fix the backward 3 even when she was tired.

Sense of Direction, *continued*

To make a 4 she said, "I'm sitting on the ruler. I slide down a little way and go straight out. I stop. Then I leap up in the air and slide down the pole part."

Lindy taught her teachers that an image must be anchored to a permanent marker, like her ruler, in a manner that is meaningful for the individual student. When visual imagery is unstable, the student needs a permanent physical anchor. Later, Lindy could use a line on the left side of her desk for a direction reference and eventually even the margin line on her tablet. Lindy also taught her teachers the importance of visualizing the entire image of her movement as she formed the number. Her language needed to describe a starting place, anchor movement to the image, and carry the motion to completion.

Strategies

1. **Teach cursive writing early.** Cursive writing provides fewer opportunities for directional problems than printing. For example, a cursive "b" is easier to recall than a printed "b" because the cursive letter has more distinctive features than just directionality. With some scripts the starting point for a cursive "d" is different from the starting point for a "b," making the two letters seem more distinct. The writing motion itself and the self-directing language for making these two cursive letters are different. Notice also that other letter pairs, such as "f" and "t," "k" and "x," "u" and "h" or "n," and "w" and "m," are easier to distinguish in cursive than in print. When directional problems are pronounced, it may help to skip printing and go straight to cursive writing.

2. **Rehearse in three dimensions.** If a student cannot understand directions while using drawings and maps, it is usually easier to leave the two-dimensional world of print and move the task to the three-dimensional world. The student can practice manipulating a three-dimensional model of land features while talking through physical relationships between objects, such as a mountain and a river.

3. **Teach the language of directions.** Teaching direction words such as *up* and *down*, *vertical* and *horizontal*, *diagonal*, *left* and *right*, *beside*, and *parallel* is important. (See the "Say Where" game in Appendix 5, pages 147-148.) Attach images to these words. For example, *diagonal* can be represented as a fishing pole or *perpendicular* as a flag pole.

Sense of Direction, *continued*

Students who demonstrate pronounced directional confusion need a permanent anchor or marker to use for defining direction such as a wristwatch always worn on the left arm. Color codes are helpful, such as a strip of red tape (red = right) down the right edge of the desk.

4. **Teach letters and numbers with a story and picture.** For example, a "b" looks like a boy kicking a ball toward the writing hand (away for left-handers). The story and the picture cue memory for the correct letter form and direction. (See Symbol Stabilization in Appendix 1, pages 129-135.)

Chapter 15: Spatial Relations

Spatial relations include qualities like size, distance, order, time, and relationships between objects, events, and ideas. Spatial thinking is important for the analysis of ideas in print and is, therefore, a potential underlying problem of some poor readers. Spatial problems manifest themselves through various combinations of behaviors.

As a toddler, Janice was verbally precocious. She understood and expressed an extensive vocabulary at age one and whole sentences by 18 months. At age eight her problems became noticeable. She had trouble organizing and arranging her things, although she could follow her mother's guidance and example in most everyday tasks like getting ready for school. Time had little meaning for her. Phrases like "in an hour" were confusing. At age twelve, she had trouble with poetry, grammar, and art. Her drawings looked like the scrawls of a very young child.

Once she was expected to write organized essays, school seemed harder for Janice. Typically, her essays were disorganized, and she had no plan for an essay before writing it. Her papers also appeared messy because she did not attend to the appropriate placement of sentences on a page. Sometimes she began writing far down the page. Simple math was difficult because she did not line up the problems correctly. Janice could not read music unless she heard it first. Socially she was criticized because she got in other people's space. For example, when the teacher was trying to work with other people, Janice would pull at the teacher's arm.

Larry was sixteen. His school bus arrived at 7:20 A.M. He had to see 7:15 on the digital clock to know that he needed to go to the bus stop. If he did not notice 7:15 on the clock, he did not understand that he had missed the bus when the clock had moved past the arrival time to 7:25.

Larry drove a car, but he had problems finding locations. He could not read a map. If he got off his usual route to a familiar place, he could not retrace his steps to find his way, even if he was only a block away from his familiar route. Upon seeing the red taillights of stopped cars ahead, he commented to his passenger that people who stop in the road deserved to be hit. When asked about the damage that an accident would do to his own car, Larry was surprised. He did not realize until it was pointed out to him that if he hit another car, the other car would hit him too! Amazingly he did not cause accidents, but his driving was limited to neighborhood errands.

Larry played junior varsity football and did all right at tight end, catching short passes. He was very fast, which offset his difficulty remembering plays. When he was assigned to return long kickoffs, he was unsuccessful. If Larry did get his hands on the ball, he was unable to read formations and did not escape the defensive players coming at him.

Larry's management of his own life can only be described as loose. His room was messy; his schoolwork was disorganized; and he was always late. None of that bothered him.

Sara, age seven, was in second grade. She was having trouble understanding specific phrases like "after dinner" and "below sea level" in reading and discussions. She did not work independently. The teacher had to tell her to do each step of a task. Sara was forever asking what she should do next, and she sometimes looked anxious when she did not know what was going to happen.

Typically Sara did not get her things put away before recess. At the end of recess, she was not ready to come in because she did not understand that 20 minutes had passed. She also did not notice the cues that recess had ended, such as students running into the building. Sara was reckless on the jungle gym. In fact, she had accidents frequently.

Mark, age ten, was in fourth grade. He was extremely shy. While all the other boys played soccer, he stood by and watched for a long time before he ran in to play. Ever since he ran to the wrong base once in softball, Mark was very cautious. He would never climb the jungle gym.

Other boys pushed Mark to the back of the lunch line because he did not defend his position in line and because he was easy to pick on. He seldom reacted to others, although at times he overreacted. He hit a boy for just bumping him after four other boys had already bumped him with no consequences.

Mark's teachers described him as "buttoned down." He was highly organized, insisting that everything be in the right place in his desk and that his papers be neat. He said that his parents told him how to do things right. They bought him a computer so that his schoolwork could be printed out to look perfect. However, when he worked in class rather than at home, he placed periods and commas randomly in his writing, read through punctuation markers orally without noticing them, and confused even the simplest math problems.

These students exhibit many markers of spatial relations problems. They have trouble with the arrangement of their physical environment, with the detection of relationships between ideas in their reading, and with the location of their bodies in space. They stand too close or talk too loud, and they violate other people's space in many ways. They have trouble with time because time is a spatial concept. In fact, clocks translate time in a spatial format segmented in intervals

Spatial Relations, *continued*

like inch marks on a ruler. These students are often confused by expressions such as "next month," "last week," and "in an hour."

Janice is a good example. Many of the tasks that were difficult for her have a spatial component, such as organizing her space, understanding time, and structuring language through grammar. Drawing and arranging her writing on a page were also difficult spatial tasks for her.

Students like Janice usually read and write poorly and have problems with particular kinds of print. They can be too literal in their understanding and miss inference, irony, satire, and humor. Poetry is exceptionally difficult. To understand this type of print, the reader must detect underlying meaning from indirect suggestion or from language expressing the opposite of what one means (irony). Layers of understanding often must be visualized spatially in the mind. Oblique inferential humor can be a mystery to people with spatial deficits, while direct and obvious slapstick may seem hilarious. Inability to grasp inference shows up in reading interpretation. People with spatial problems are often unable to draw their own conclusions beyond what they see in print.

Janice had a problem with social skills related to spatial understanding. She violated other people's physical space, appearing clumsy and socially maladroit. She would stand too close to people and speak in a voice that was too loud.

Larry also illustrated many spatial problems. He had trouble perceiving the position of his car in space accurately which caused him to get lost or have accidents. He could not track and catch a football traveling a long distance, and he misunderstood the running patterns represented by football plays. He lived a disordered life with things everywhere in his room and his desk a mess. He also had trouble arriving on time.

Students with spatial problems sometimes appear to adopt a casual attitude toward their sloppiness like Larry. Others focus too much on order like Mark, whose parents helped him organize and demanded that he do so. Mark was exceptionally orderly and neat when doing work at home under parental influence. However, without parental support in the classroom, his spatial problems with organization, grammar, and math became evident.

Sara had severe problems with time and space which resulted in constant difficulty with being on time and understanding what she should be doing next, a source of anxiety for her. She did not understand the consequences of high climbing on the jungle gym. In fact, understanding cause and effect in the physical world and in text is difficult for many students with spatial problems.

Some Indicators of Spatial Problems

- difficulty with math: learning facts, "seeing" the problem and answering easily, lining up problems on a page, visualizing manipulations, shifting from + to x, understanding place value, borrowing, division, fractions, algebra

- forgetting or reversing symbols, such as letters, numbers, and codes; mixing up b/d, h/y; mixing up letters in words

- trouble drawing or copying a design, rotating or reversing drawings

- frustration putting together puzzles, seeing easily the whole from parts and how shapes fit together

- handwriting problems, such as learning cursive; uncertainty about how to form some letters, reversals, sloppiness, running words together on a page

- grammar errors, such as leaving out the subject or the verb

- capitalization and punctuation errors, the latter being markers of pauses in time

- trouble understanding words that relate ideas, such as *before*, *with*, *if/then*

- difficulty telling time using a regular clock which represents time passing with hands moving in space

- difficulty with other forms of measurement such as length and volume

- difficulty organizing/scheduling activities in time

- getting lost in a building, mall, parking lot, or neighborhood

Some Indicators of Spatial Problems, *continued*

- trouble reading a map or giving accurate and comprehensible directions to someone else

- disorganization in space; losing things; having a messy desk, locker, or room

- problems organizing written work and oral reports; difficulty visualizing the logical order of a presentation

- failing to see cause and effect, the consequences of actions which can lead to social problems

- acting out when frustrated with spatial tasks in school or at home

- failing to see things spatially or perhaps socially from another person's point of view

- intruding on others' space, interrupting, frequently "in-your-face"

- tuning out when asked to hold ideas and mentally manipulate them

- difficulty self-monitoring academic work by remembering at intervals to check for errors

- difficulty reading music notes on a staff

Note: Any single individual may have different combinations of these problems, but usually not all of them. The variation may be due to differences in ability or to compensation strategies used. Note also that many of these markers occur in persons with directional confusion or dyslexia. Both of these conditions typically include spatial problems.

Spatial Relations, *continued*

There are two categories of spatial understanding—visual-spatial and motor-spatial. Visual-spatial performance is using sight to discriminate differences and determine where to move. Motor-spatial performance is using the body and the movement of the body as a referent to understand relationships in space. A good basketball player feels the relationship between body and hoop. This is motor-spatial skill. Handwriting requires both visual and motor skill—knowing where to send the pencil and being able to make it go there. (See Chapter 3: Handwriting and Motor Skills, pages 37-46.) Many activities demand a combination of the two skills.

The Effect of Spatial Skills on Reading

Often people with spatial problems have difficulty abstracting a central idea and imposing their own order on what they read through questioning, paraphrasing, and rearranging print. Organizing a reply to an essay question requires the spatial ordering of concepts. Not knowing where or how to start is a frequent complaint of students with spatial problems. They do not easily conjure up an idea or image, look at it flexibly in different ways, analyze it, and synthesize a response. Spatial planning supports reading analysis.

People can compensate for poor spatial skills by following verbal rules for analysis. But people who do this often hold onto their language rules rigidly, without the understanding necessary for flexible thought.

Reading comprehension often relies on the spatial cues of analogy and parallels. The spatially disabled reader may miss these cues and only grasp concrete meanings. He usually decodes better than he comprehends. As a result, an apparently successful reader at a primary age may suddenly seem to demonstrate a comprehension problem later as the demands for reading analysis increase. Actually the problem was always there, but analogy and spatial language are emphasized to a greater degree in upper elementary and secondary school. A drop in reading scores in later grades indicates a potential spatial relations problem.

Spatial relations problems affect reading and writing in other ways. Punctuation puts the spaces of oral language into written form. Marks that show relationship, such as apostrophes, may be difficult to grasp for the student with spatial problems. Expressions of relationships are also difficult, such as grammar terms like verb, noun, and pronoun. Problems with expressions of location, shape, quantity, direction, interval, time, and movement are often evident in students with spatial disorders.

Spatial Relations, *continued*

Strategies

1. **Teach spatial relations in the three-dimensional world.** Students need to learn to image spatial relations through direct instruction. They should start with the three-dimensional world and practice spatial relationships that they can see and manipulate. For example, they can create visual analogies such as cylinder is to cube as circle is to square. They can manipulate objects and draw arrows in the direction of the relationships.

2. **Teach scripts for spatial tasks.** Teachers can teach students to use scripts to handle specific problems. That is, they can rehearse specific phrases with students that will guide them through tasks. For example, if students confuse + and x in math, they can be taught to ask a friend to mark all the +'s yellow so that they can recognize them.

   Eventually students should learn to script themselves and figure out how to initiate the script. They can tell themselves, "I'm adding fractions. I'm going to end up with a bigger number. First I do this..." Students need to recognize when a script is needed and work with the teacher or friend to make one up. One caution is not to make the script too narrow. The student needs to be able to generalize to other situations. A rigid script can restrict the problem solving approaches available to the student.

3. **Anticipate spatial demands in academic tasks.** Teachers can watch out for extra difficulty created by the nature of their assignments. For example, some students have difficulty copying assignments from the board, whereas the same assignment on paper at the student's desk may present few problems. The teacher can be extra careful of maps, directions, organization requirements in the classroom and on paper, visual tracking requirements, grammar, and relating two concepts or ideas in reading. Horizontal lines representing positive and negative numbers are a puzzle to some of these students, whereas, a vertical line like a thermometer may feel more naturally positive and negative.

4. **Use oral language to orient students.** Students with severe spatial problems often have difficulty visualizing spatial environments or events described in print. Reading aloud to students with these problems is important. Often words can become the means to capture spatial reality.

Parents should talk them through their spatial environment and identify visual markers to orient them. For example, while driving, a parent can point to some visual marker and say, "Mount St. Helens is over there so we are going south." These students need talk to build spatial comprehension of their environment and of their reading when they do not come to this understanding easily themselves.

5. **Help students understand their disability.** Students need to understand their disabilities and how to compensate. When they get discouraged by negative comments on their language mechanics, they need to tell themselves, "Remember that grammar is spatial." They need to watch for the spatial component of tasks throughout their lives.

6. **Help students learn to organize.** Teachers and parents can teach these students to organize themselves by making lists and thinking about what will be needed prior to doing particular tasks. Since they do not visualize planning steps in their heads easily, they have to write down and post their plans, such as the three things to do before leaving school to go home. Students can thus use language to direct themselves and compensate for spatial problems. The teacher can also model organizing tools, like a box for individual art supplies.

7. **Provide visual cues for time.** Some students (such as Janice) do not image a day, and they wonder where they are in the day and what will happen next. A student can understand where he is in the school day if he has a time line taped to his desktop. As the class day progresses, he can move a paper clip along the time line or mark off segments of the time line with colored pens. The time line can be divided into equally-sized segments representing 15 minutes each and labeled with activities during the day, such as reading or recess. Different activities can be indicated with different colors. Another good way to experience time passing is to observe the process with a sand timer.

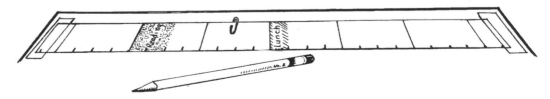

8. **Remediate grammar physically.** Grammar problems can be remedied with a Sentence Builders/Word Shapes approach, which allows students to manipulate syntactic elements represented by plastic shapes. (See Appendix 2, pages 136-142.) As far as commas and periods are concerned, the ear can also tell some students where to place marks indicating pauses. Sometimes indicating comma placement with gestures is helpful. In an exercise designed to raise awareness of comma placement, the student claps for each word and thrusts his fist forward at a pause that would then need a comma. The student might say, "The swimmers kick hard, and the water is deep," while going "clap-clap-clap-clap-thrust-clap-clap-clap-clap-clap."

9. **Recognize barriers to drawing.** If the student who scrawls really needs to draw, the teacher can teach a few stereotypic drawing techniques, such as triangular evergreen trees. This is purely an expediency to increase comfort level with drawing and to help avoid embarrassment in school.

10. **Help students align work on paper.** Give graph paper for math, lined paper for writing, and worksheets with the positions of headings and indentations indicated.

11. **Teach sequence through imagery.** To make sequence stand out in print, teach students to attach images to key points in the narrative. The images can be real objects, pictures, notes, or pictures in the mind, with the latter being a goal that might be reached through practice with external cues first. Students then recount sequences from these images.

Another technique is to work with the student to mark key words in a story that indicate events in a sequence. The student can then step back and tell the sequence from the key words and even practice changing around the sequence.

Some kinds of text are easier to read for sequence. Narrative is easy because it is like a conversation. High action narrative is easiest because the images are vivid. The reader can miss a great deal and still get the story line. Science text usually has simple syntax, although the vocabulary might be new. It is easier to read content that is already familiar to the student, such as stories about special interests like auto mechanics or football.

Spatial Relations, *continued*

12. **Create physical referents for common measures.** Teach distance by marking an inch high on the finger and a foot long on the student's arm. Then the student can use these body clues to understand measurement in space. To help the reckless student like Sara on the jungle gym, create a parallel experience for the effect of falling. Have the student drop a soft ball of dough or clay from different heights. When the dough gets flat on one side from falling, the student can understand that he has climbed too high.

13. **Enlist parental support.** When a child like Mark is unsuccessful and anxious about moving his body in space, enlist the parents' support. Parents can help children adjust to space gradually, not just throw them into a swimming pool when they are afraid to jump in. Talking through such actions allows the child to use language to explain what are otherwise puzzling or frightening spatial relationships.

    Spatial problems create a sense of being lost—lost in text, in space, or in knowing what to do next. Appropriate support can enhance achievement and self-confidence for students with spatial problems.

    (For more information about spatial relations, contact this website: **http://www.newhorizons.org/spneeds_arkspatial.html**.)

Part III:

Appendices—Teaching Tools

Appendix 1: Symbol Stabilization

Some students struggle with letter memory. They are unsure of how to configure letters, forming them differently each time. They may confuse letter direction, mixing up "b/d" or "y/h." They spell inaccurately, and their writing may be slow and inefficient.

Symbol stabilization is a training procedure involving several exercises to build clearer and more accurate memories for letters. The approach focuses on the distinctive features of letters and includes multisensory learning as well as techniques for offsetting directional confusion. Multisensory learning involves multiple senses in the learning process, such as hearing, seeing, and feeling letters. It creates multiple associations and many routes to access material in memory.

The following intervention activities help students with learning disabilities form stable memories for letters. These activities may be used as needed to solve individual letter recall problems. The distinctive features exercises should be done first.

- identifying letters by their distinctive features alone
- tactually identifying three-dimensional letters
- tactually identifying two-dimensional letters
- composing stories to reduce directional confusion
- making picture notes to sharpen visual distinctiveness

Identifying letters from their distinctive features. Distinctive features are the minimal parts of a letter that must be present for a person to recognize the letter. For example, the distinctive feature of "e" is ⊃ because that is really all that one must notice to recognize "e." No matter how much one alters "e" with fancy print, "e" can be recognized if its distinctive feature is there. Most people know and recognize letters from their distinctive features automatically, but some students need help to learn this.

There are a variety of ways to practice recognizing and using distinctive features of letters. The teacher can lay out distinctive feature cards and ask the student to identify the corresponding letters. The teacher can lay tracing paper over letter grids and ask the student to indicate on the tracing paper the distinctive features of the letters showing through. The sheet of letters on page 131 can be used with the student to mark distinctive features. It can also be cut into separate letter pieces for exercises.

Symbol Stabilization, *continued*

The teacher can discuss the letters the student does not know and have the student feel plastic letters and raised letter cards for recognition. The feeling exercises can be done in the context of discussion about distinctive features, answering questions like "Why do you think it's a 'b'?"

Distinctive features marked on an alphabet:

a b c d e f g h i j k l m

n o p q r s t u v w x y z

"Write-on" slides for a standard projector can be used to practice letter recognition from distinctive features. The distinctive features of a letter are drawn on a slide. At first only one letter is put on a slide, then two, and then three. Eventually each slide will have up to four letters. The student practices recognizing letters when they are displayed for a split second. After the quick presentation of each slide, the student names the letters she saw on the slide and writes them down. After the total presentation, the student goes back over the slides slowly, checking and discussing her performance with the teacher.

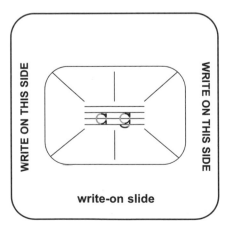

model for
drawing
distinctive
features on
slides

a b c d e

f g h i j k l

m n o p q

r s t u v w

x y z

Mark the distinctive
features on each letter.

Symbol Stabilization, *continued*

Guidelines for using distinctive features:

1. All practice, including exercises with slides, is done at normal reading distance.

2. The letter groups displayed in distinctive feature form are those naturally found in words.

3. Students must initially learn accurate standard features that distinguish letters.

4. These features are then described in the student's language to assure specificity of features and the ability of the student to sort and sift features orally.

5. The features are displayed to the student only for a moment so as to require the student to scan her afterimage for the array before responding, just as successful readers do with print.

6. The student both says and writes the letters represented by the distinctive features displayed.

Tactually identifying three-dimensional letters. Heap several lowercase alphabets of plastic letters on a tray. Ask the student to sort out an alphabet from this pile of letters. This allows the teacher to watch the student select letters to see the ease or difficulty of this task. After the student sorts the letters visually, the teacher puts one or two of them in a cloth bag. The teacher then asks the student to put her hand in the bag and identify the letter by touching it. If the student is right-handed, she uses her left hand for this task. The student also describes what her  fingers are telling her. Tactile memory typically stimulates visual images. The student needs to rehearse until she understands the process of touching the letter, calling out the name, and then pulling out the letter to confirm her label. The teacher then puts a larger group or even the entire alphabet into the bag, and the student proceeds to tactually identify the letters.

Note: If the student does not have the language to describe the letters, the teacher can present the letters visually and have the student arrange them in descriptive groups such as tall/short, round/not round, and letters that hang down/those which do not. (See also Appendix 5, pages 147-150.)

Symbol Stabilization, *continued*

The entire set of letters is sent home with the student and she is directed to use her left hand, feel the entire letter, and say its name two or more times a day. Soon the student can instantly identify each of the letters she has practiced. The assignment may be amended to include writing the letter with one hand while feeling it with the other.

A box with cuffs can be used for tactile letter identification instead of a bag. This allows the teacher to observe children as they touch each letter and call out its name. Some children use a scattered or haphazard approach to tracing the letter with their fingers. Others impulsively call out a letter name after touching only part of the letter. Children who have attention disorders or motor-planning problems are especially inefficient at letter identification. Their handwriting tends to be jerky and impulsive. For them, copying letters is non-reflective and usually fails to reinforce visual memory.

After a few days of these exercises, the student can usually identify letters very rapidly. Often the student can identify the entire alphabet within two or three minutes. Her tactual image has sharpened. Because tactual images influence visual images, students often report changes at this stage in how letters "look" to them.

Tactually identifying two-dimensional letters. This exercise is more demanding than identifying three-dimensional letters and typically would follow as a next step. Commercially prepared raised letters on cards are made from a textured substance such as sandpaper or bumpy plastic. Teachers can also make their own letter cards by using glue or fabric paint. A hole is punched in each card, and the cards are put on a ring for convenience. The student holds the card in one hand and runs the fingertips of her non-writing hand along the letter to identify it and call out its name.

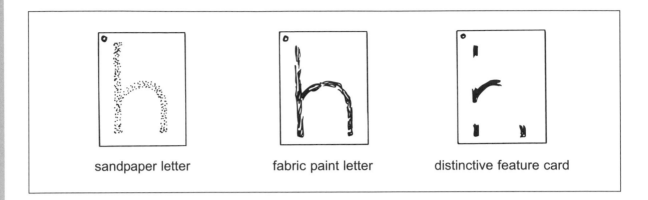

sandpaper letter   fabric paint letter   distinctive feature card

Composing alphabet stories. This procedure is reserved for the most troublesome letters. For each letter that a student cannot label, a story is composed that stimulates recall of the letter name. For example, if the student cannot remember the name for "r," the letter can be turned into a stick figure with an arm. *Arm* sounds like "r" and triggers the name of the letter.

For students who have particular trouble with direction, the story should link direction with the name of the letter. For example, a "b" can be drawn as a boy with a soccer ball that is kicked toward the writing hand (away from the writing hand with a left-handed student). A "d" can be drawn as a dog with a tail behind it. The dog faces toward the writing hand of a right-handed student and away from the writing hand of a left-handed student.

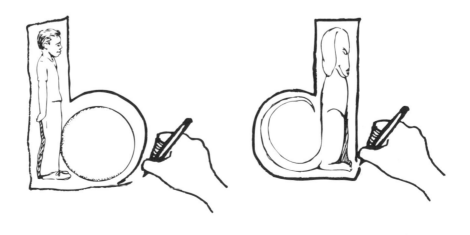

Symbol Stabilization, *continued*

Making picture notes to sharpen visual distinctiveness. Some students need to use their own cues to remember differences. "That's an 'f,'" said one student, "because its neck bends like a giraffe." The teacher suggested that the letter looked like a candy cane. With his seven-year-old wisdom, the student said, "A candy cane could turn either way, but a giraffe would work okay." His own imagery features worked better to reduce directional confusion than those the teacher suggested. After drawing his picture note, he never confused "f" again. The process of creating the note and describing the link he meant to establish fixed the directional features of the letter in his memory.

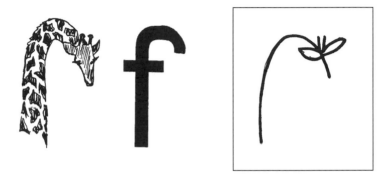

Students who demonstrate profound directional confusion may need a combination of several activities to assure firm and accurate letter memories.

Appendix 2: Sentence Builders/Word Shapes

Word Shapes are plastic shapes that can be manipulated to represent parts of speech and syntactic patterns. Through practice manipulating these shapes to build sentence patterns, the student learns the rules of sentence structure. This is a visual representation of syntax, which simplifies learning for people with language problems.

Word Shapes illustrate:

- the function of each word in a sentence

- different sentence patterns

- complete and incomplete sentences

- clauses and phrases

- active and passive sentences

- how the same word can be used for different functions

- when punctuation marks such as commas are needed

- how to combine sentences

- how to rearrange words in sentences to create questions

- foreign language patterns

Word Shapes represent parts of speech.
Combining Word Shapes illustrates grammar.
Word Shapes exercises help students understand how
language structure conveys meaning.

Word Shapes can be purchased from:
ARK Foundation   Phone: (253) 573-0311
Allenmore Medical Center   Fax: (253) 573-0211
1901 S. Union   Ste. A311   E-mail: ARKFdn@aol.com
Tacoma, WA 98405

Word Shapes (pieces for creating the sentence patterns of language)

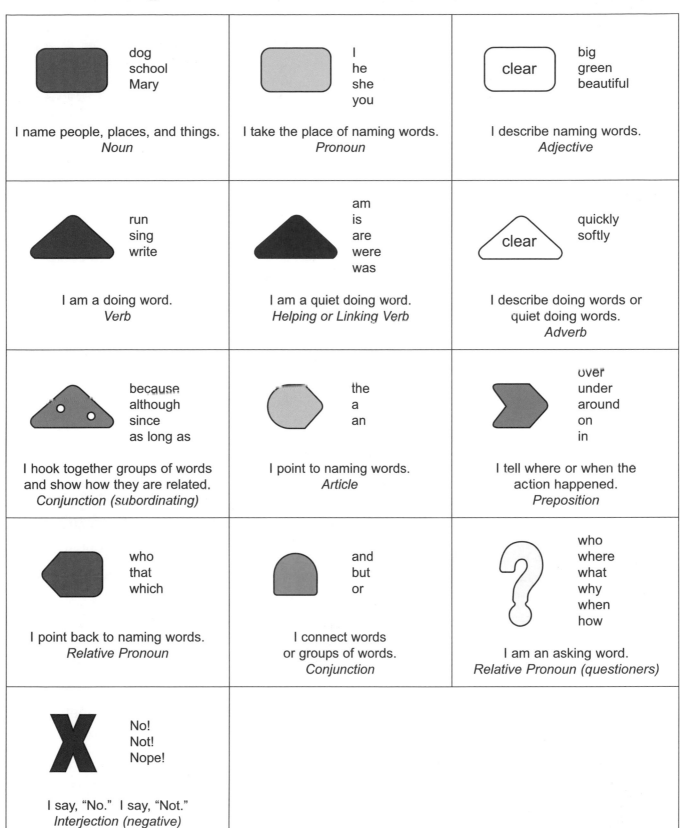

dog
school
Mary

I name people, places, and things.
Noun

I
he
she
you

I take the place of naming words.
Pronoun

clear
big
green
beautiful

I describe naming words.
Adjective

run
sing
write

I am a doing word.
Verb

am
is
are
were
was

I am a quiet doing word.
Helping or Linking Verb

clear
quickly
softly

I describe doing words or
quiet doing words.
Adverb

because
although
since
as long as

I hook together groups of words
and show how they are related.
Conjunction (subordinating)

the
a
an

I point to naming words.
Article

over
under
around
on
in

I tell where or when the
action happened.
Preposition

who
that
which

I point back to naming words.
Relative Pronoun

and
but
or

I connect words
or groups of words.
Conjunction

who
where
what
why
when
how

I am an asking word.
Relative Pronoun (questioners)

No!
Not!
Nope!

I say, "No." I say, "Not."
Interjection (negative)

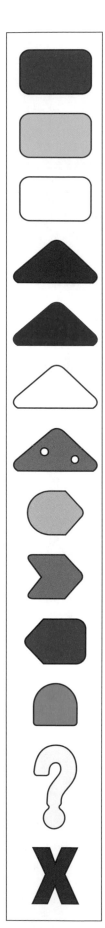

Word Shapes, *continued*

Syntax Exercises

The following sequence of exercises helps the student understand language structure. The pieces can be manipulated to expand and practice syntax in a variety of ways. It is unnecessary to label the shapes as parts of speech such as "verb." Instead, one can label the word's function in a sentence such as "doing word."

Finding the Focus of a Sentence

The focus is the actor (subject) and its action (verb). The student can place the blue ▬ on the actor and the red ▲ on the action in a picture. He can then be asked to say what is "blue" (actor) and "red" (action) in the picture. This same exercise can be done with sentences.

Practice with Simple Sentences

The student can practice making symbol strings to represent a picture with only one actor and one action. For example, presented with a picture of a cow in a field, the student can say the sentence and then construct the following string with the symbol shapes:

The student can then construct several similar sentences to rehearse this pattern.

If the teacher rearranges the symbols, the student can practice variations in word order such as, "In the shower, the man sang." Students see that the same meaning can be expressed with a different word order. Also, various arrangements that do or do not work soon make it apparent that order is important for meaning and the smooth flow of a sentence. The student quickly sees that some pieces go together in phrases such as "in the shower." For homework, the student can compose simple sentences and reorder these sentences.

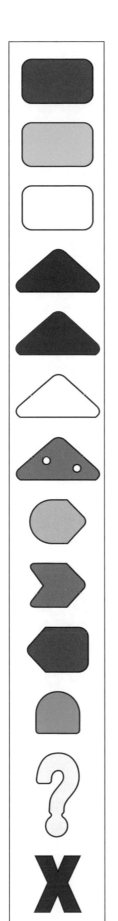

Word Shapes, *continued*

Forming a Question

The teacher can demonstrate to the student that rearranging the order of words and their symbol pieces can form a question. Then the teacher can ask the student to rearrange pieces to form questions with other symbol strings. For example, the following sentence is presented.

The student is asked to move the pieces to form a question.

In another exercise, placing the question mark on one piece in a symbol string cues the student to form a question asking for that item as an answer. For example, placing the question mark on the shape for "boy" in the above symbol string cues the question, "Who is swimming across the lake?" The question mark piece is then substituted for the boy piece to visually demonstrate that specific questions call for particular items of information. This demonstration is very important because students often do not understand that question words call for particular types of answers.

Combining Sentences Using Connecting Words

Another exercise is combining two simple sentences to form one sentence using words and symbol pieces. Some examples:

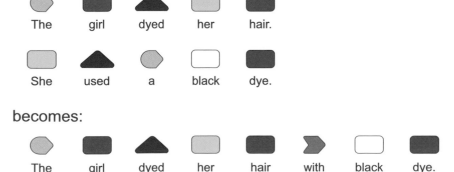

becomes:

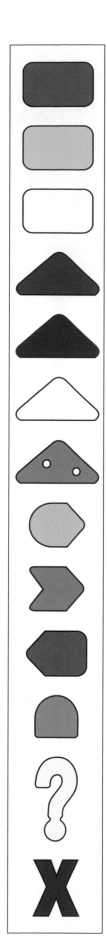

Word Shapes, *continued*

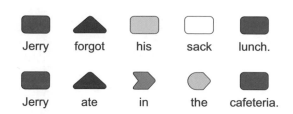

Jerry forgot his sack lunch.

Jerry ate in the cafeteria.

becomes:

Jerry, who forgot his sack lunch, ate in the cafeteria.

The student may compose the two simple sentences himself and combine them, or the teacher may compose the two sentences for the student to combine. When the teacher composes the two sentences, usually writing them before the learning session is more efficient.

Other Types of Sentences

A compound sentence can be represented visually with the ⬭ shape linking the symbol pieces representing two simple sentences. Through practice manipulating symbols for this pattern, the student sees that a compound sentence contains the shapes for two nouns and two verbs. For example,

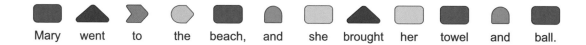

Mary went to the beach, and she brought her towel and ball.

For a relative clause, the teacher might present a motivating picture such as an array of desserts and model the symbol string.

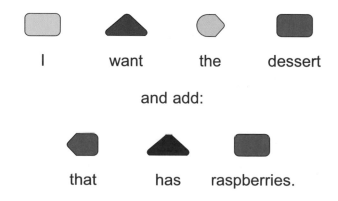

I want the dessert

and add:

that has raspberries.

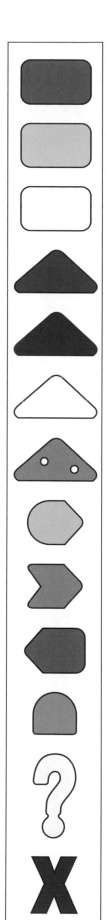

Word Shapes, *continued*

The student quickly realizes that the relative clause is necessary to specify the dessert that he wants. The student can add relative clauses referring to the other desserts.

For additional practice, the student can combine sentences by using relative clauses. The student should practice this with words and symbol pieces.

Some example sentences are:

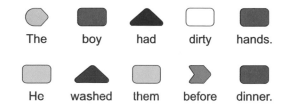

becomes:

The student constructs questions in the "what" pattern.

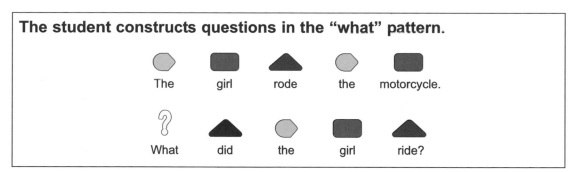

The student constructs questions in the "where" pattern.

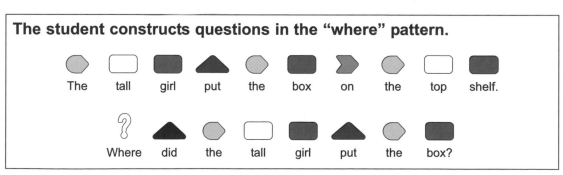

Word Shapes, *continued*

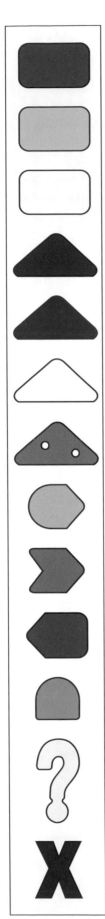

The student constructs questions in the "when" pattern.

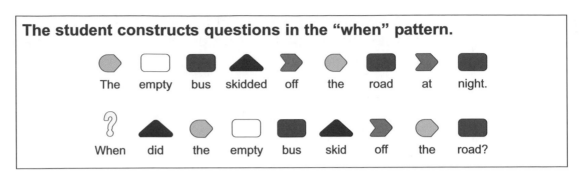

The empty bus skidded off the road at night.

When did the empty bus skid off the road?

The student creates and amends various constructions.

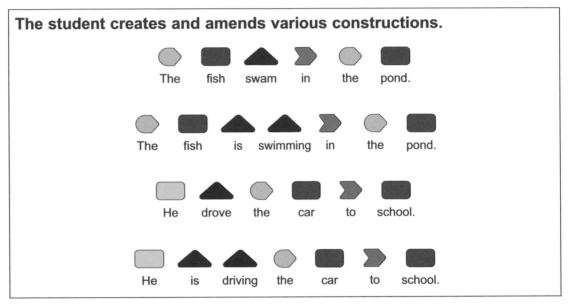

The fish swam in the pond.

The fish is swimming in the pond.

He drove the car to school.

He is driving the car to school.

Finally, the student can practice recognizing simple, compound, and complex sentences if the teacher presents example sentences on cards and asks him to categorize the cards according to the type of sentence pattern. The student can recognize these patterns in print with instructions to find a compound sentence or a simple sentence.

The order of the above suggestions can be altered. However, in general, the teacher needs to keep in mind the order of learning difficulty. Sentence production with teacher cues is easier than sentence production without them. Also, seeing a pattern in a string of symbol pieces is far easier than when the same task is in print.

Appendix 3: Picture Notes—A Memory Strategy

In order to remember something, one must visualize it accurately, noticing the distinctive features that set it apart from any similar item. If one does not image the key features, that is, the essence of the item to be remembered, then memory is vague and elusive. Noticing and remembering key features applies to learning letters, words, pictures, paragraphs, and even textbook chapters, as illustrated by examples throughout this book. This strategy is useful for remembering abstract ideas as well as concrete objects. Imaging key features is a powerful tool for recall.

Picture notes directly facilitate the imaging process. Drawing the note forces the learner to identify and clarify the distinctive features to be learned. Also, the note itself forms associations in memory that trigger recall.

The picture note is a rapid sketch of distinctive features to remember. Artistic skill is unimportant. All that is important is that the learner records the image of key features to recall.

Steps for Teaching Picture Noting

Identify distinctive features. Accurate images incorporate distinctive features, those that distinguish an item from other similar items and are essential for understanding.

Talk about the features. Language helps clarify distinctive features and provides labels, another avenue for recall.

Start with one object. Talk about what you see. Student and teacher both draw notes. Examine and compare notes.

Draw notes for several objects. Evaluate. Do the notes distinguish between the objects? If not, discuss the distinctive features that differentiate the objects. Draw the notes again.

Draw notes for pictures.

Draw notes for print. Use narrative print first, then other forms of text.

Draw notes for an event, then for several events, and finally for a newscast of events.

PICTURE NOTES

A TOOL TO SHAPE & RECALL IMAGES

The essence of an image can be captured in a picture note.
Clarifying the image makes evident the information to be learned.
The process of creating the picture note reinforces memory.

OVERVIEW

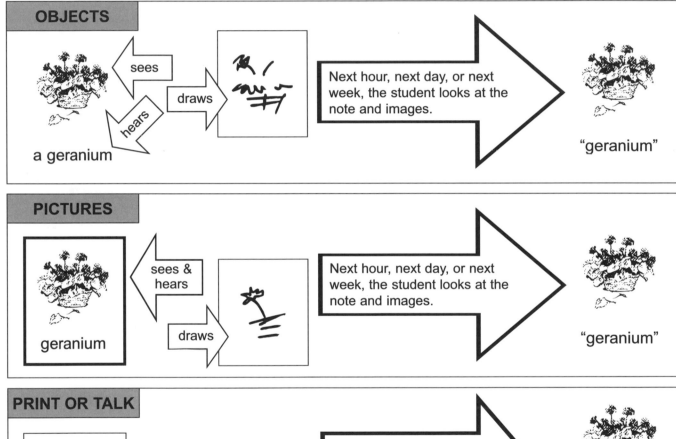

OBJECTS

sees

hears

draws

a geranium

Next hour, next day, or next week, the student looks at the note and images.

"geranium"

PICTURES

geranium

sees & hears

draws

Next hour, next day, or next week, the student looks at the note and images.

"geranium"

PRINT OR TALK

"Those flowers are called geraniums. Geraniums are popular flowers with red, white, or pink blossoms."

sees & hears

draws

Next hour, next day, or next week, the student looks at the note and recalls that geraniums are flowers. Perhaps the student will also recall color details and that they are sometimes planted in a basket.

"Oh, I know. Geraniums are flowers. They might have pink or white or red blossoms."

Appendix 4: Junk Box

📖 ## Using Classification As A Tool to Specify Image and Language

This exercise helps build vocabulary and sharpen word understanding. If a student has trouble extracting the essential features of word meaning, instruction and rehearsal in categorization is helpful. Categorizing requires an examination and selection of features to use in sorting. For example, one can sort by categories like shape, color, size, or use.

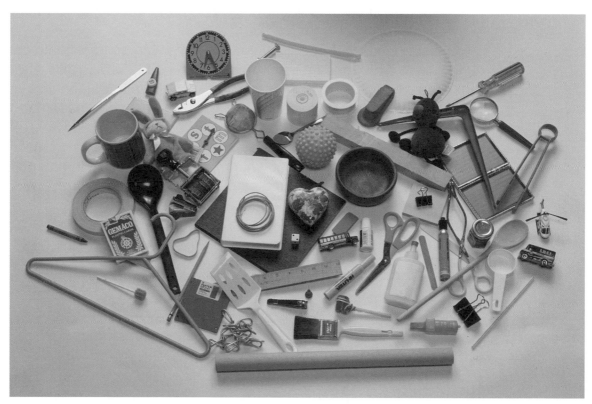

An array of junk

A modeled category

The junk box exercise provides opportunities to categorize. The student sorts and sifts through a pile of items on a table as the teacher models a simple category such as shape. The teacher encourages the student with conversation during the process. A student might say, "That's not cloth. It's round things. The balls go here too. I suppose some things just don't fit into any pile."

Junk Box, *continued*

The teacher may need to help with categorization clues—"Okay, so this is the cloth or leather pile; this is the plastic pile; this is the paper pile." Then the student is usually able to classify the rest.

The teacher and student discuss which feature to use for classification, noting that there is more than one possibility. Then the student sorts the objects again using different categories. The teacher and student should discuss why some things fit into a category and other things do not. This sorting process forces the student to identify essential features of items. This discussion allows a student to enrich and specify word meanings.

A guessing game affords additional practice with specific features of words. One player describes an item according to its features, while the other guesses which item is being described. As the player identifies multiple features of objects, he expands and embellishes word meanings.

The junk box is an easy game that expands vocabulary and makes it more specific. It is a reminder that words are easier to learn in categories. Much of memory is arranged around categories of meaning. Learning lists of un-related vocabulary words is unnecessarily difficult.

Appendix 5: Teaching Games

SAY WHERE

A Game That Teaches the Vocabulary of Direction and Position

Equipment for each player:
- a folder
- blocks
- a square or rectangle of paper that is used as a base sheet

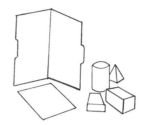

Rules:

One person is "It."

"It" gives directions while placing the game pieces on his base sheet. For example, "I am placing my small red square on the center of the blue square."

All players try to follow these oral instructions with their own base sheets and game pieces while their moves are hidden behind their folders as a screen. If the leader gives unclear instructions, the other players will quickly **demand** greater clarity of word choice. Players' understanding of the words they hear will be apparent in how they place their blocks. They will self-correct as play continues. At the end of his "turn," "It" removes his folder and everyone compares block arrangements.

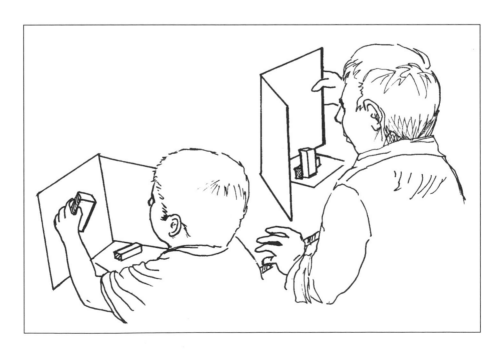

Teaching Games, *continued*

Variations:

- The number of players can range from two to a classroom. Teams of two or three players can work together to place the blocks. Their discussion of choices helps them build firmer understanding of the oral directions.

- The number of blocks can vary from one to many. However, each player must have identical blocks. Starting with a single rectangular block helps players build common meanings for *top*, *flat*, *up*, and so on.

- A line, square, circle, or triangle may be drawn on the base sheet so that players must consider this in their block placements.

- Objects such as a pencil, marble, or ruler may be included and placed according to oral instructions by "It."

- Selected words such as *horizontal* or *diagonal* may be required language for a game. Eventually *left*, *right*, *east*, *west*, *north*, and *south* can be included.

The game is fast moving!

Teaching Games, *continued*

THE HAND GAME

A Game Which Reinforces Memory for Letter Shape and Position by Motor Movement

The players' hand positions illustrate the placement of letters such as on the line, hanging below the line, or rising above the line.

Rules:

"It" is the leader who calls out letters. The leader's hand positions illustrate the letters as each one is called. The leader may make hand movements with the players or slightly after them to allow the players opportunity to respond. Players may be an entire class or one or two students plus the leader. Change the player who is "It" frequently. Use this game for brief five- or six-minute periods as a warm-up exercise.

Hands Up	**Hands Down**	**Fist**
b d f h k l t	g j p q y	a c e i m n o r s u v w x z
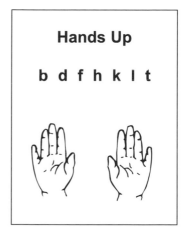	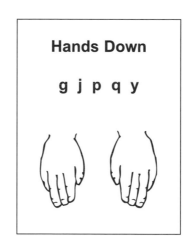	

a	g	t	u	o	j
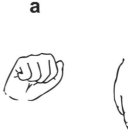					

BASKETBALL PLAYERS
An Image to Reinforce the Position of Letters

Put each letter of the alphabet with the basketball player that matches its position on the line.

_____

_____

_____

Annotated Bibliography

TOPIC AREAS:

Brain & Mind
Children's Development
Imagery, Perception, & Visual Thinking
Intelligence
Language and Speech
Learning Disabilities & Attention Disorders
Memory
Reading, Writing, Spelling, Mathematics, & Literacy
Special Needs
Structures & Systems

BRAIN & MIND

Calvin, W. H. *The Throwing Madonna*. New York, NY: McGraw-Hill Book Company, 1983. This book by University of Washington neurologist Calvin includes essays on many subjects such as handedness, strokes, language development, and pain.

Campbell, J. *The Improbable Machine*. New York, NY: Simon & Schuster, Inc., 1989. Campbell explores the various comparisons of the mind to the computer and says they are based on the incorrect premise that the mind is a logic machine. Instead he claims that the mind is based on experience as the controlling feature.

Campbell, J. *Winston Churchill's Afternoon Nap*. New York, NY: Simon & Schuster, Inc., 1986. The author describes how we perceive time and the implications of temporal awareness in our lives.

Corballis, M. C. *Human Laterality*. New York, NY: Academic Press, 1983. The author examines laterality from many different perspectives and applies that information to conditions such as dyslexia and stuttering.

Damasio, A. R., M.D. *Descartes' Error*. New York, NY: G. P. Putnam's Sons, 1994. Damasio's University of Iowa laboratory is a widely recognized center for study of brain-damaged patients. This book explores the physical substructure of feelings.

Dobkin, B. H., M.D. *Brain Matters: Stories of a Neurologist and His Patients*. New York, NY: Crown Publishers, Inc., 1986. The author presents personal narratives that cover a wide range of neurological conditions.

Annotated Bibliography, *continued*

Gardner, H. *The Shattered Mind*. New York, NY: Vintage Books, 1976. Dr. Gardner describes the impact of various forms of brain injury and the insight into brain function that these patients provide.

Gazzaniga, M. S. & LeDoux, J. E. *The Integrated Mind*. New York, NY: Plenum Press, 1979. This book responds to those authors who emphasize right and left hemisphere function by rejecting many narrow interpretations in favor of looking at the function of the entire brain.

Gazzaniga, M. S. *Mind Matters*. Boston, MA: Houghton Mifflin Company, 1988. The author describes how the mind and brain are linked together and the effect of this linkage on many conditions from "pain to passion, from depression to delirium, from anxiety to addiction."

Gazzaniga, M. S. *The Social Brain*. New York, NY: Basic Books, Inc., 1985. The author emphasizes the social nature of the brain as it unifies the many "modules" of processing to create a unified consciousness.

Gregory, R. L. *Eye and Brain*, 3rd Ed. New York, NY: McGraw-Hill Book Company, 1978. This widely used, authoritative book describes eyesight, perception, and vision.

Hooper, J. & Teresi, D. *The 3-Pound Universe*. New York, NY: Dell Publishing Company, Inc., 1986. The authors range broadly over many aspects of brain research and theory. They describe the human brain as the last great frontier: "The brain is the only organ given the task of studying itself."

Luria, A. R. *The Working Brain: An Introduction to Neuropsychology*. New York, NY: Penguin Books, Ltd., 1973. In this book the Russian psychologist, Aleksandr Romanovich Luria, describes functional systems of operation within the brain. His lifelong research led to significantly broadening our understanding of the brain as interactive working systems. He was a pioneer in neuropsychology.

Penfield, W. & Roberts, L. *Speech and Brain-Mechanisms*. Princeton, NJ: Princeton University Press, 1959. This pioneering work describes the mechanisms of speech from a research neurologist's viewpoint.

Pribram, K. H. *Brain and Perception: Holonomy and Structure in Figural Processing*. Hillsdale, NJ: Lawrence Erlbaum Associates, 1991. This book records the 1990 John M. MacEachran Memorial Lectures at the University of Alberta. The subtitle denotes the content.

Restak, R., M.D. *The Brain, the Last Frontier*. New York, NY: Warner Books, Inc., 1980. The author conveys how the brain functions as a base of emotion, language, and thought.

Restak, R., M.D. *The Brain Has a Mind of Its Own*. New York, NY: Crown Publishers, Inc., 1991. The author is a practicing neurologist who presents many vignettes as short glimpses that portray the interrelationship of mind and brain.

Restak, R., M.D. *Receptors*. New York, NY: Bantam Books, 1994. The author describes current knowledge of the brain centering on the function of neurotransmitters. He also presents the impact of drugs on these chemical linkages as help for patients who have Parkinson's, schizophrenia, or many other disorders.

Taylor, G. R. *The Natural History of the Mind*. New York, NY: Penguin Books, 1981. The author is a British science writer who explains brain function from perception to consciousness, from typical processes to disease processes. He focuses as well on "thinking about thinking."

CHILDREN'S DEVELOPMENT

Ault, R. *Children's Cognitive Development*, 2nd Ed. New York, NY: Oxford University Press, 1983. The author examines children's cognitive development from both Piagetian and experimental child psychology viewpoints. Piaget is presented as a stage theory addressing specific areas while non-Piagetian theory focuses on quantitative change within processes.

Bower, T. G. R. *The Perceptual World of the Child*. Cambridge, MA: Harvard University Press, 1979. This small book describes infants' perceptual abilities and their development as portrayed by a series of experiments. The young child has a far more complex and functioning perceptual system than previously thought.

Bruner, J. *Child's Talk*. New York, NY: W. W. Norton & Company, Inc., 1983. The author describes when and how children acquire language and explains what may help them do so. Dr. Bruner suggests that children have a "language acquisition support system" that mediates the developmental processes of language.

Goodnow, J. *Children Drawing*. Cambridge, MA: Harvard University Press, 1977. This book from the *Developing Child Series* investigates child art because, in the words of the author, "children's drawings present the world from the point of view of the child."

Annotated Bibliography, continued

Kellogg, R. *Analyzing Children's Art*. Palo Alto, CA: Mayfield Publishing Company, 1970. This illustrated book traces children's artistic development. The reader learns to identify the predictable stages that occur in children throughout the world.

Lowenfeld, V. & Brittain, W. L. *Creative and Mental Growth*, 5th Ed. New York, NY: The Macmillan Company, 1970. This is a significant art education textbook encompassing the role of art and art instruction in human growth and development.

Wadsworth, B. J. *Piaget for the Classroom Teacher*. New York, NY: Longman, Inc., 1978. The author is a psychology professor who set out to make the concepts and philosophy of Piaget understandable and practical for classroom teachers and students of education.

IMAGERY, PERCEPTION, & VISUAL THINKING

Arnheim, R. *Visual Thinking*. Los Angeles, CA: University of California Press, 1969. The processes of vision involve thinking and reasoning. Perception, in Arnheim's view, is the stuff of thinking, through which we structure events and derive ideas. "The language of images is a prime mover of the constructive, creative imagination. Thinking calls for images and images contain thought." Dr. Arnheim was Professor Emeritus of Psychology of Art at Harvard at the time he wrote this book.

Barlow, H. C. Blakemore & Weston-Smith, M. *Images and Understanding*. Cambridge, MA: Cambridge University Press, 1990. The editors present a comprehensive collection of papers on the form, function, and processes involved with imaging. They convey how images help make meaning and participate in thought.

Bloomer, C. M. *Principles of Visual Perception*. New York, NY: Van Nostrand Reinhold Company, 1976. The author explains and illustrates the mechanisms of visual perception.

Dondis, D. A. *A Primer of Visual Literacy*. Cambridge, MA: The MIT Press, 1973. The author describes the essential skills needed to create and to understand visual communication.

Epstein, W. & Rogers, S. (eds.) *Perception of Space and Motion*. San Diego, CA: Academic Press, 1995. The authors present current information about the application of perception in a variety of situations that include depth, pictorial layout, events, and three-dimensional structure as well as the development of space and motor perception.

Annotated Bibliography, *continued*

Gombrich, E. H. *Art and Illusion*. Princeton, NJ: Princeton University Press, 1969. The author originally presented these ideas at the A. W. Mellon Lectures in Fine Arts at Princeton. The theme of the work is: "A study in the psychology of pictorial representation."

Jackendoff, R. S. *Languages of the Mind: Essays on Mental Representation*. Cambridge, MA: The MIT Press, 1993. These essays investigate mental representation of widely different content including spatial information.

Kosslyn, S. M. *Ghosts in the Mind's Machine*. New York, NY: W. W. Norton & Company, 1983. The author explores how humans create and use images in the brain.

Kosslyn, S. M. *Image and Mind*. Cambridge, MA: Harvard University Press, 1980. This author explores imagery, how images are created and used, and makes a case for the central role of images in the function of the mind.

McKim, R. H. *Experiences in Visual Thinking*. Monterey, CA: Brooks/Cole Publishing Company, 1972. This is a Stanford University textbook used in the course on visual thinking developed by the author.

McKim, R. H. *Thinking Visually*. Belmont, CA: Lifetime Learning Publications, 1980. This strategy manual for problem solving includes a wide range of exercises to help individuals learn to solve visual problems.

Pick, A. D. (ed.) *Perception and Its Development: A Tribute to Eleanor J. Gibson*. Hillsdale, NJ: Lawrence Erlbaum Associates, 1979. The authors present a series of papers that portray the nature and development of perception.

Potegal, M. (ed.) *Spatial Abilities, Development and Physiological Foundations*. New York, NY: Academic Press, 1982. The authors examine the way organisms learn to understand spatial relationships and review the physiological and neurological mechanisms involved.

Samuels, M., M.D. & Samuels, N. *Seeing with the Mind's Eye*. New York, NY: Random House, 1980. This comprehensive book explores the history, techniques, and uses of visualization.

Schone, H. *Spatial Orientation: The Spatial Control of Behavior in Animals and Man*. Princeton, NJ: Princeton University Press, 1984. This book describes how animals orient themselves in space as well as the mechanisms and processes involved.

Scientific American Readings. *Perception: Mechanisms and Models.* San Francisco, CA: W. H. Freeman and Company, 1972. This collection of articles includes fundamental research papers on perception, systems, and processes.

INTELLIGENCE

Kaufman, A. S. *Intelligent Testing With the WISC-R.* New York, NY: John Wiley & Sons, 1979. Professor of educational psychology and trainer of psychologists, Kaufman is concerned with appropriate use of measurement devices, especially the WISC-R. He helped Wechsler revise this instrument. In this technical book, he describes many patterns and discrepancies that provide greater insight into test performance.

Khalfa, J. (ed.) *What Is Intelligence?* Victoria, Australia: The Cambridge University Press, 1994. This book records the Darwin College Lectures which investigate many aspects of intelligence ranging from enhancing intelligence to the language of intelligence to visual processing links.

Salvia, J. & Ysseldyke, J. E. *Assessment in Special and Remedial Education*, 2nd Ed. Boston, MA: Houghton Mifflin Company, 1981. This is a comprehensive textbook for "those whose careers require understanding and informed use of assessment data." The authors describe, analyze, and criticize many tests providing insight into valid and reliable test data. They also evaluate test manuals.

LANGUAGE & SPEECH

Beveridge, M. & Conti-Ramsden, G. *Children with Language Disabilities.* Milton Keynes, England: Open University Press, 1987. The authors describe the impact of various types of language disability and set forth markers to help educators and parents recognize the problems.

Bower, B. "Language Without Rules." *Science News*, 14, pp. 346-347, 1994. Bower describes the hereditary factors in language disorders.

Bloom, P., Peterson, M. A., Nadel, L., & Garrett, M. F. (ed.) *Language and Space.* Cambridge, MA.: The MIT Press, 1996. This book emanated from a conference that sought to answer questions such as: How do we represent space? and What role does culture play in spatial representation? The authors investigate orientation and left/right confusion.

Annotated Bibliography, continued

Bruck, M. "Persistence of a Dyslexic's Phonological Awareness Deficits." *Developmental Psychology*, 28(5), pp. 874-886, 1992. People with dyslexia do not acquire appropriate levels of phoneme awareness, regardless of their age or reading levels.

Campbell, J. *Grammatical Man.* New York, NY: Simon & Schuster, Inc., 1982. Language and the concepts of information theory are the focus of this book. Campbell says, "The human being is the most complex communications network on earth, and language is a code which preserves the orderly structure of the messages of speech in ways so ingenious that they are still not fully understood."

Catts, H. "Speech Production/Phonological Deficits in Reading-Disordered Children." *Journal of Learning Disabilities*, 19, pp. 504-508, 1986. This viewpoint is the basis for combined instruction in speech, language, and reading.

Catts, H. "The Relationship Between Speech-Language Impairments and Reading Disabilities." *Journal of Speech and Hearing Research*, 36, pp. 948-958, 1983. This information supports combined instruction in speech, language, and reading.

dc Villiers, P. A. & J. G. *Early Language.* Cambridge, MA: Harvard University Press, 1980. This book from the *Developing Child Series* describes how language develops from birth to school age.

Elliot, A. J. *Child Language.* Cambridge, England: Cambridge University Press, 1980. From the Cambridge Textbooks in Linguistics, this author focuses on the way children learn language. She surveys research, including Piaget and Chomsky, as well as other current studies.

Eng, T. & Hellige, J. "Hemispheric Asymmetry for Processing Unpronounceable and Pronounceable Letter Trigrams." *Brain and Language*, 46, pp. 517-535, 1994. This information is the basis for teaching only letter combinations which actually occur in words.

Garvey, C. *Children's Talk.* Cambridge, MA: Harvard University Press, 1984. This book from the *Developing Child Series* fully describes the process and purposes of language development.

Hunr, R., Elliott, J., & Spence, M. "Independent Effects of Process and Structure on Encoding." *Journal of Experimental Psychology: Human Learning and Memory*, 4, pp. 339-347, 1979. These authors describe the relationship between language structure and reading.

Jonas, G. *Stuttering*. New York, NY: Farrar, Straus and Giroux, 1977. This small book is written by an ex-stutterer who investigated the diverse theories and therapies in use.

Kamhi, A. G., Pollock, K. E., & Harris, J. L. (eds.) *Communication Development and Disorders in African American Children: Research, Assessment, and Intervention*. Baltimore, MD: Paul H. Brookes Publishing Co., 1996. The authors investigate a wide range of issues that affect the language of African American children and the social and cultural understanding of those issues.

Kamhi, A. & Catts, H. "Toward an Understanding of Developmental Language and Reading Disorders." *Journal of Speech and Hearing Disorders*, 51, pp. 337-347, 1986. This article describes the relationship between language development and reading.

Lewis, B. "Familial Phonological Disorders: Four Pedigrees." *Journal of Speech and Hearing Disorders*, 55, pp. 160-170, 1990. The author describes the hereditary factors in phonological disorders.

Orlando, J. & Bartel, N. R. "Cognitive Strategy Training: An Intervention Model for Parents of Children with Learning Disabilities." *Journal of Reading, Writing, and Learning Disabilities International*, 5, pp. 327-344, 1989.

Paul, R. & Shriberg, L. "Associations Between Phonology and Syntax in Speech-Delayed Children." *Journal of Speech and Hearing Research*, 25, pp. 536-547, 1982. A language linkage pertinent to reading instruction is described.

Schwartz, R., Leonard, L., Folger, M., & Wilcox, M. "Early Phonological Behavior in Normal-Speaking and Language Disordered Children: Evidence for a Synergistic View of Linguistic Disorders." *Journal of Speech and Hearing Disorders*, 45, pp. 357-377, 1980. The early evidence of links between various aspects of language performance is described.

Scruggs, T. & Mastropieri, M. "Classroom Applications of Mnemonic Instruction: Acquisition, Maintenance, and Generalization." *Exceptional Children*, 58, pp. 219-229, 1992. This article explains the use of imagery and language cues.

Vygotsky, L. & Kozulin, A. (eds.) *Thought and Language*. Cambridge, MA: The MIT Press, 1987. The editors revised and edited a seminal work by Vygotsky, a Russian psychologist (d.1934) who investigated the development of language and thought in children. He was an intellectual colleague of Luria.

Annotated Bibliography, *continued*

LEARNING DISABILITIES & ATTENTION DISORDERS

Gaddes, W. H. & Edgell, D. *Learning Disabilities and Brain Function*, 3rd Ed. New York, N.Y.: Springer-Verlag, Inc., 1994. This book is a bridge between the neurology of the brain, the biology of learning, and the practical issues of learning. The authors tried to write for a general reader rather than a medical researcher.

Hartmann, T. *Attention Deficit Disorder: A Different Perception.* Penn Valley, CA: Underwood-Miller, 1993. The author uses the metaphor "a hunter in a farmer's world" to portray the daily life of ADD children and adults. He focuses on ADD not as a disability, but as a difference which may even be an asset.

Levine, M. D., M.D. *Developmental Variation and Learning Disorders.* Cambridge, MA: Educators Publishing Service, Inc., 1987. Dr. Levine is professor of pediatrics at the University of North Carolina School of Medicine as well as director of the Clinical Center for the Study of Development and Learning. This comprehensive book explores a huge field ranging from developmental variation to medical conditions in relation to academic procedures, social, and emotional growth. Topics include dysgraphia, depression, memory, and mnemonic strategies.

Lyon, G. R. (ed.) *Frames of Reference for the Assessment of Learning Disabilities.* Baltimore, MA: Paul H. Brookes Publishing Company, 1994.

Lyon, G. R., Gray, D. B., Kavanagh, J. F., & Krasnegor, N. A. (eds.) *Better Understanding Learning Disabilities.* Baltimore, MA: Paul H. Brookes Publishing Company, 1993. The editors assembled chapters from many of the leading figures in medicine and education to portray the current understanding of this field.

Rourke, B. P. (ed.) *Syndrome of Nonverbal Learning Disabilities.* New York, NY: The Guilford Press, 1995. This book has chapters on various children's diseases and dysfunctions that all include non-language-centered learning disability. Rourke presents a white-matter model of NLD.

Schwarz, J. *Another Door to Learning.* New York, NY: The Crossroad Publishing Company, 1992. Eleven short stories portray and personalize language and spatial learning disabilities. The stories illustrate what needs to happen for learning to occur.

Smith, S. L. *No Easy Answers: The Learning Disabled Child at Home and at School.* New York, NY: Bantam Books, 1987. This book surveys the entire field of learning disabilities and provides practical recommendations for parents and educators.

Smith, S. L. *Succeeding Against the Odds: How the Learning Disabled Can Realize Their Promise.* New York, NY: Jeremy P. Tarcher/ Perigee, 1991. The subtitle also describes the contents.

MEMORY

Kail, R. *The Development of Memory in Children.* San Francisco, CA: W. H. Freeman and Company, 1979. Memory, according to Kail, is a collection of processes rather than a single entity. Children's memory systems develop in orderly and predictable fashions and are related to other cognitive development.

Luria, A. R. *The Mind of a Mnemonist.* Cambridge, MA: Harvard University Press, 1968. Dr. Luria tells the story of a young man with an apparently limitless memory whom he studied over a period of many years. His words describe how memory works.

Luria, A. R. *The Man with a Shattered World: The History of a Brain Wound.* Cambridge, MA: Harvard University Press, 1972. Dr.Luria tells the story of "a person who fought with the tenacity of the damned to recover the use of his damaged brain."

Rosenfield, I., M.D. *The Invention of Memory.* New York, NY: Basic Books, 1988. The author makes a case **against** the theory of localization of brain function or against any form of fixed storage. He postulates that the brain is organized into a category-creating system and describes how such a system relates to perception, vision, and memory.

Squire, L. R. *Memory and Brain.* New York, NY: Oxford University Press, 1995. This psychiatrist reviews memory research up to this time and charts the different ideas that have been put forth. In the section on synaptic change, he describes the ways in which synapses could hypothetically change as a result of learning. Squire writes: "forgetting reflects an actual loss of information from storage and synaptic changes in areas that stored the information. Memory is regional and distributed—many parts of the memory system participate in the memory of a single event. We have multiple working memories or a collection of temporary capacities."

READING, WRITING, SPELLING, MATHEMATICS, & LITERACY

Bettelheim, B. and Zelan, K. *On Learning to Read: The Child's Fascination with Meaning.* New York, NY: Vintage Books, 1982. The authors address the critical period between kindergarten and third grade.

Kozol, J. *Illiterate America.* New York, NY: New American Library, 1985. Kozol presents a compelling picture of the prevalence and impact of illiteracy. He notes "one in three Americans cannot read the pages of this book."

Miles, T. R. and Miles, E. *Help for Dyslexic Children.* London, England: Methuen, 1983. These Welsh authors were early advocates of direct instruction for dyslexic students.

Pavlidis, G. T. and Fisher, D. F. (eds.) *Dyslexia: Its Neuropsychology and Treatment.* New York, NY: John Wiley & Sons, Ltd., 1986. The editors compiled research from medicine and education to present a detailed review of current knowledge regarding identification and instruction of dyslexic individuals.

Slobin, D. I. *Psycholinguistics*, 2nd Ed. Palo Alto, CA: Scott, Foresman and Company, 1979. This book refines and further explores the psycholinguistic theory of language first presented a decade earlier.

Smith, F. *Reading Without Nonsense.* New York, NY: Teachers College Press, 1978. Dr. Smith writes about reading from the psycholinguistic perspective that he helped develop. He worked as a newspaper reporter, magazine editor, and novelist before his best known efforts as a researcher in language education and the psychology of learning.

Smith, F. *Understanding Reading: A Psycholinguistic Analysis of Reading and Learning to Read*, 3rd Ed. New York, NY: Holt, Rinehart, and Winston, 1982. Smith presents reading as a language activity.

Stiggins, R. J. *Student-Centered Classroom Assessment.* Upper Saddle River, NJ: Prentice-Hall, Inc., 1997. The author describes procedures for monitoring student progress in reading and writing within the classroom.

SPECIAL NEEDS

Dorris, M. *The Broken Cord.* New York, NY: Harper Perennial, 1990. This narrative about a young boy afflicted with Fetal Alcohol Syndrome describes the impact of the condition and day-to-day needs of the child, his family, and the people who seek to help him.

Ehrlich, V. Z. *Gifted Children: A Guide for Parents and Teachers.* Englewood Cliffs, NJ: Prentice-Hall, Inc, 1982. The author writes as a parent in addition to her role as professor and research coordinator of the Astor Program for gifted children at Columbia University.

Annotated Bibliography, continued

Fraiberg, S. *Insights From the Blind.* New York, NY: New American Library, 1977. The book subtitle "Comparative Studies of Blind and Sighted Infants" describes the growth and development of children blind from birth.

Kitano, M. K. & Kirby, D. F. *Gifted Education, A Comprehensive View.* Boston, MA: Little, Brown and Company, 1986. This textbook covers many topics related to gifted individuals: identification, instructional programs, family considerations, needs, and subgroups of gifted, such as learning disabled.

Padden, C. & Humphries, T. *Deaf in America.* Cambridge, MA: Harvard University Press, 1988. The authors, who are themselves deaf, describe the nature of deaf culture, the central role of sign language, and the misunderstandings of the hearing world.

Robinson, K. *Children of Silence: The Story of My Daughters' Triumph Over Deafness.* New York, NY: Penguin Books, 1991. The author narrates the experiences of a family with two young girls who have severe hearing impairments.

Sacks, O. *Seeing Voices: A Journey into the World of the Deaf.* Los Angeles, CA: The University of California Press, 1989. The author explores the history of deaf people in the United States, deaf culture, deaf communication, and the ideas that dominate opposing groups.

STRUCTURES & SYSTEMS

Belasco, J. *Teaching the Elephant to Dance.* New York, NY: A Plume Book, 1991. The author describes how to embrace change and to manage an organization successfully to accomplish its vision. The organization may be a business, a school, or other agency.

Dyson, F. *Infinite In All Directions.* New York, NY: Harper & Row, Publishers, 1989. The author is a physicist who probes science, philosophy, and religion in a wide ranging book designed to provoke thought about the physical, intellectual, and spiritual universes.

Rubin, S. E. *Public Schools Should Learn to Ski: A Systems Approach to Education.* Milwaukee, WI: ASQC Quality Press, 1994. The author introduces two models for restructuring schools to function as systems.

Index

Abstract question
67
ADHD
104
Alphabet stories
134
Attention
31, 49, 56, 66, 103-108,
133, 159
Auditory discrimination
109, 110
Auditory memory
29, 31, 109

Basketball player(s)
122, 150

Categorize
87, 142, 145
Categorizing
87, 96, 145
Complex language
85, 102
Control scale
49, 50
Cue(s)/Cueing
51, 52, 54, 79, 94-96, 98, 100,
101, 104-106, 110, 114, 116,
118, 122, 124, 125, 135, 139,
142, 158
Cursive
37, 39, 42, 115, 120

D'Nealian
37
Decode(s)/Decoding
10, 11, 19, 22, 47, 49, 86, 122
Direction(s)/Directional
29, 43, 46, 48, 75, 78, 89, 99,
106, 114-116, 121-123, 129,
134, 135, 147, 148
Distinctive feature(s)
9, 23, 67, 75, 79, 81, 88, 95,
102, 111, 114, 115, 129-132,
134, 143
Dysgraphic
38, 46
Dyslexia
39, 121, 151, 157, 161

Empower(s)/Empowered/
Empowerment
54, 55
Executive function(s)
47, 49
External cue(s)/cueing
11-14, 17, 19, 20, 22, 51, 52,
98, 101, 105, 125

Grammar
9, 74, 83, 84, 99, 117, 119,
120, 122-125, 136

Hand game
149
Handwriting
30, 31, 34, 37-46, 120, 122,
133
Hatchet words
33
Health factors
104
Hearing examination
110

Image(s)
9, 11, 13, 23, 32, 39, 41,
42, 48, 61, 62, 67, 73-81,
89, 90, 95, 96, 112, 113,
115, 122-125, 132, 133,
143-145, 150, 154, 155
Imagery
33, 40, 42, 56, 61, 67, 73-81,
92, 112, 115, 125, 135, 154,
155, 158
Imaging objects
79
Imaging pictures
81
Inferential
55, 66, 94, 98, 119
Inferential question
66
Internal cue(s)/cueing
11, 12, 14-17, 27, 47, 51

Junk box
87, 145, 146

Keyboarding
33, 46

Language development
9, 83, 151, 157, 158
Language features
84, 113
Language system
82
Language window
43
Learning progression
17
Literal
55, 57, 58, 61, 66, 98, 119
Literal question
66

Monster word(s)
34, 35, 113
Motor memory
30, 31, 37, 38, 113
Motor-planning behaviors
41
Multisensory
94-96, 100, 110, 129

Organization
53, 68, 119, 123

Perspective taking
59
Phonics
19, 23, 25, 27, 32, 39, 110
Picture note(s)
18, 19, 23-25, 33, 45, 48, 51,
62, 66, 67, 75, 78, 79, 81, 88,
89, 95, 107, 108, 110, 112,
129, 135, 143, 144
Picture noting
75, 79, 81, 82, 88, 112, 143
Plot point
61
Progression
17, 27, 44

Index, *continued*

Rating sheet
54, 106
Reading level(s)
10-12, 98, 157
Research/Researching
64, 67-69, 91, 156
Rote
57, 58, 73, 92, 94
Rote learning
57

Script(s)
37, 39, 42, 43, 60, 89, 90,
106-108, 114, 115, 123
Scripting
82, 89
Self-talk
53, 83
Semantics
84, 90, 91-97
Sentence combining
100
Sequence(s)/Sequencing
13, 38, 41, 47, 48, 52, 54, 55,
62, 86, 89, 90, 96, 100, 103,
110, 118, 119, 121, 125, 138
Snake in the jar
64, 65
Spaced practice
34, 45, 113
Spatial problems
39, 41, 42, 96, 117, 119,
120-124, 126
Spatial relations
96, 114, 117-126
Spatial relationships
155
Speech factors
110
Spelling
20, 22-24, 28-36, 39, 42,
45, 46, 91, 109, 119, 160
Spelling box
34-36
Spelling notebook
34, 36
Spelling strategies
31, 34, 36, 113
Stopping language
102

Studying for tests
66
Symbol Stabilization
19, 112, 113, 116, 129-135
Syntax
10, 11, 15, 84-86, 90, 97-102,
125, 136, 138, 158

Tactile memory
132
Tactual/Tactually
129, 132, 133
Teaching games
147-150
Three-dimensional letter(s)
113, 129, 132, 133
Two-dimensional letters
129, 133

Unsticking readers
15, 16

Visual cue(s)
10, 94, 96, 124
Visual discrimination
111-113
Visual memory
22, 23, 29, 31, 39, 111-113,
133
Visual phonics
23, 25, 27, 110
Vocabulary
9-14, 18, 27, 42, 57, 67, 73-75,
78, 81-89, 91-97, 99, 105, 109,
117, 125, 145-147

Web/Webbing
1, 94, 97
Website
135
Word families
26, 32, 96
Word segmentation
29, 31, 110
Word Shapes/Sentence Builders
97, 100, 101, 125, 136-142

19-01-987654321